Country Decorating with Fabric Crafts

Books by Leslie Linsley

Leslie Linsley's Night Before Christmas Craft Book
Leslie Linsley's Christmas Ornaments and Stockings
America's Favorite Quilts
Million Dollar Projects From the 5 & 10¢ Store
Making It Personal With Monograms, Initials and Names
The Great Bazaar
Army Navy Surplus: A Decorating Source
Afghans to Knit & Crochet
Quick and Easy Knit & Crochet
Custom Made
Wildcrafts
The Decoupage Workshop
Decoupage: A New Look at an Old Craft
Decoupage for Young Crafters
Air Crafts
Fabulous Furniture Decorations
New Ideas for Old Furniture
Photocraft
Scrimshaw

Country Decorating
with
Fabric Crafts

by Leslie Linsley

Design and photography by Jon Aron

St. Martin's/Marek

Design by Jon Aron

Library of Congress Cataloging in Publication Data

Linsley, Leslie.
      Country decorating with fabric crafts.

      1. Textile crafts. 2. Interior decoration—Amateurs'
manual.   I. Title.
TT699.L56   1985   646.2′1   85-1720
ISBN 0–312–17035–1

First Edition
10 9 8 7 6 5 4 3 2 1

Photographs on pages 43, 47, and 89
courtesy of *Family Circle* magazine.

Acknowledgments

My appreciation is extended to the
manufacturers who have been helpful in the
preparation of this book. Their cooperation and
interest in furnishing their beautiful materials
for the purpose of designing the projects have
been most generous.
They are:
  VIP Fabrics, New York, New York
  Stacy Fabrics Corp., Wood Ridge,
    New Jersey
  Laura Ashley Fabrics, New York, New York
  Fabrications, Newton, Massachusetts

I am especially grateful to Robby Smith for her
creative contributions and to Lawrence Kane for
his input on the original projects that appeared
in *Family Circle* magazine.

Contents

Country Decorating with Fabric Crafts

Introduction

Country decorating has become part of every home in America. Even city dwellers often try to incorporate a touch of the homey, country feeling in some part of their living space. If, for example, a room needs a soft, lived-in touch, a quilted wall hanging can do the trick. Sometimes it's little accents that make a dramatic difference. By adding handmade pillows to a couch, you create an interesting, warm, focal point.

We Americans take great pride in our homes and the way each room looks. We are constantly changing our environment to better serve our ways of living. Often it is difficult to make major purchases to achieve this end, but we can still have an effect on the overall look by the personal touches we add.

Most of the home accessories found in boutiques and department stores are easy to make. All that's required is some pretty fabric, trimmings, and the basic sewing skills. Home sewers usually have full baskets (or in my case a full trunk) of remnants: scraps of leftovers from projects, and yards of pretty material saved for a rainy day. It's always fun to make use of these because we can save money and the time it takes to pick out the perfect fabric for the project. Whenever possible I've tried to use small pieces of different fabrics to make up the whole. In this way you can use up the scraps you may already have on hand to make the projects included in the book.

In crafting we usually associate scraps with fabric and think of the projects as being made from pieces of material stitched together, as in patchwork, or applied over one another, as in appliqué. In fact it is these very techniques combined with a variety of small prints and warm colors that are used to achieve the country look in decorating.

If you use materials that are already on hand and apply your basic crafting skills, there are lots of ways to enhance your decor with a minimum of cost and effort. The wall hanging on page 62 with matching pillows is a good example of how you can change the look of a room with a few accessories.

The table runner and patchwork ruffled pillows on pages 67 and 70 are reminiscent of authentic early American antiques. By using a variety of small prints and light and dark colors, you can get the same country effect.

Baby quilts for carriage and crib are excellent projects to make from personal scraps. Just as this country's early settlers made quilts from old shirts, worn bed linens, and so on, you can do the same. Imagine your baby or grandchild snuggled under a coverlet made from his or her mother's graduation dress or daddy's favorite worn shirt. It adds a nostalgic sentiment to the item that can't be purchased.

There are larger projects presented here, such as the room-divider screen on page 120. Although it takes lots of fabric, the whole thing can be made of many different small pieces, which don't have to match. The square log cabin quilt on page 113 is updated with Laura Ashley fabric for a contemporary feeling applied to a traditional design.

Most of the projects are quick and easy and can be done in a few hours, but some will take several days. When working on this book I found that once the items had been designed, the directions worked out, and the projects made, I wanted to use everything. I think you'll find a good variety of ideas, styles, and techniques with many different uses for all.

General crafting how-to's

All the projects in this book are made with a variety of fabrics from everyday calico cotton prints to men's suiting material. The techniques are familiar to sewers and easy enough for the beginner to learn. The materials and directions are listed and explained with each project. However, there are some general tips and how-to's that pertain to all. The following is a summary of that information for easy referral as you work on each project. They'll also help you prepare the necessary materials in the most efficient way.

Enlarging designs and patterns

Although most of the projects have been designed so the patterns could be presented full size, occasionally it will be necessary to enlarge a design. In this case I have provided a grid and indicated the size each square represents. Usually 1 square equals 1 inch. You then transfer the design to, or copy it onto, paper marked off into 1-inch squares. You can make your own graph paper or buy a pad in an art supply store.

Transferring designs and patterns

You can transfer most of the designs from this book to another surface such as the fabric background. Simply trace the design on a sheet of tracing paper, then retrace the design on the back of the tracing paper. Place the paper over the background fabric and rub a pencil over the outlines of the design. Remove the tracing and go over the design so you can see it more clearly on the fabric.

Cutting out patterns

Take the time to determine how you will place each pattern piece on the fabric to get the most from your material. This is especially important when making multiples. For example, when making the table runner on page 67, first choose a variety of light and dark fabrics that will look good together. Decide how many of each you will need for the length of your table and cut out several layers of fabric using the one pattern piece. The number of layers to be cut at one time will depend on the type of fabric used. It's a good

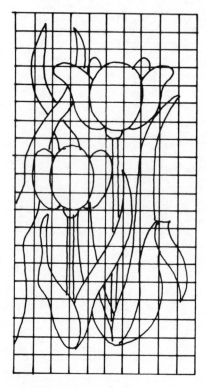

Enlarging a design

idea to use similar weight fabric for all pieces that will go into a project.

Sewing

Sewing pattern pieces in the right sequence makes a big difference in time and efficiency, as well as accuracy.

Plan thread colors so that all stitching with one

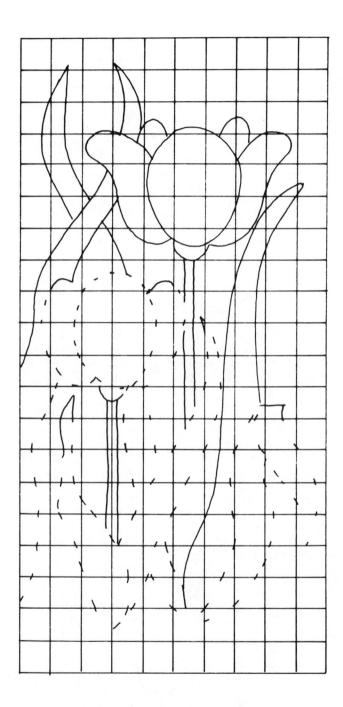

color can be done before changing spool and bobbin.

If you're working in quantity, do all the same steps on each piece at one time rather than completing one and starting the next.

Any hand or lap work such as stuffing and finishing openings should be done at one time. I like to save these finishing details to do while relaxing.

If you're working on several projects, such as the runner and the two pillows on pages 67 and 70, think through the arrangement of patch pieces so you don't end up with all of one print. You want the overall effect to be varied as well as harmonious. The braided trim can be added as the final touch. This is an enjoyable and creative activity, so save leftover scraps of lace, ribbons, buttons, and so on for the added touches.

Stacy's Stitch Witchery is used to fuse two pieces of fabric together, as with appliqué. You can buy it in strips, small packages, or by the yard. You will find it invaluable for tacking down ribbon trim, when you're in a rush and don't want to do a lot of sewing, for tacking hems, and for a million other little projects. The two collages on pages 148 and 151 are a cinch to do with this product.

Fabrics

Almost any fabric can be used for the projects in this book; however, some are easier to work with for different crafting techniques.

Muslin is a good, inexpensive backing material and is often used for country pillows such as the animal shapes on page 128. Muslin comes 45, 52, and 60 inches wide and sells for approximately $3.00 a yard.

Felt won't fray so it's good for some projects (though not all). The border for the wool coverlet on page 64 is made from felt, which gives the finished project some weight.

Polished cotton, satin, and velvet will give any of the projects an elegant look. Small overall prints like calico are good choices for small projects.

Sheets are pretty and practical for many sewn projects. If you have a floral sheet that is worn, consider cutting it up to use for appliqués. For example, the pillows on page 116 could be appliquéd with large sheet florals. A worn bed sheet is perfect for backing a quilt because it is soft from many washings. This is a good way to recycle. And since they come in twin, full, queen, and king sizes you won't have to piece the backing as you would with most 45-inch-wide fabric.

Making and using templates

If a template is needed for a project, it will appear in the book the same size for easy transfer to the fabric. To do this, trace the outline onto a sheet of tracing paper. Place this face down onto thin cardboard and rub over each traced line. The outline will come off on the cardboard. For a sharper image, place a piece of carbon paper on the cardboard with the tracing on top. Go over each line with a pencil. Remove the tracing and cut out the design outline from the cardboard. Use sharp scissors or a craft knife.

Determine which fabric will be used for each template. Figure out the best layout for getting the most pieces from your fabric. For example, place all triangles on the fabric so they form squares. Mark around each template on the fabric. Since this will be your sewing line, each piece must be cut ¼ inch larger all around for seam allowances. Place each template ½ inch apart to allow for this extra fabric. Consider the grain of the fabric when placing your templates.

Piecing

Although it is not faster, it is often easier to sew by hand. You can take your work with you or sew while relaxing. Also, some complicated designs are easier to do by hand. However, if you machine-stitch, the work will go faster and be stronger than handwork.

Sewing points

Many patchwork patterns are created from triangles, diamonds, and similar shapes. The

16

points present a challenge and require special care.

When stitching two such pieces together, sew along the stitch line but do not sew into the seam allowance at each point. It helps to mark the finished points with a pin so you can begin and end your seams at these marks.

Appliqué tips

When applying one fabric to another, as with the projects on pages 21 and 22, you can use a matching thread or a contrasting one to define the appliquéd shapes. Pin or baste the shapes in place on the fabric. You can then use an invisible hemming stitch or overcast the edges with embroidery floss. If you simply fuse the pattern to the background fabric, you will want to go around the outline with a zigzag stitch on your machine.

Tools

Scissors: If you invest in good-quality scissors from the start, they will be the best investment you'll ever make. A good pair of scissors can cut a straight line of fabric without fraying or pulling it. Do not use them for anything but cutting fabric. If you cut paper with your fabric scissors, they will not perform as well again.

It's also a good idea to have a small pair of snipping scissors handy. These will be invaluable for hand or machine stitching. In our house someone is always yelling, "Where are the scissors?" so I have several pair —and still I can't find the snipping scissors two seconds after I use them! I've found that if you tie a ribbon to them you'll keep track of them more easily.

Ruler: A metal ruler is invaluable for marking straight edges and a yardstick for most measuring. You may prefer a tape measure, but I tend to lose mine, and a yardstick is large enough to be visible at all times. Besides, you can also use it to mark straight lines, even though it isn't as accurate as the metal ruler.

Basic stitches

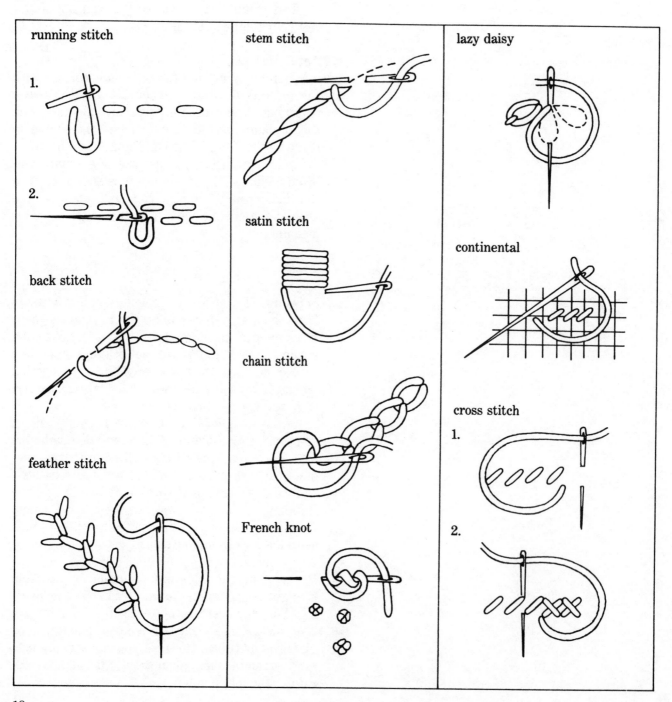

running stitch

1.

2.

back stitch

feather stitch

stem stitch

satin stitch

chain stitch

French knot

lazy daisy

continental

cross stitch

1.

2.

Appliqué

Appliqué is the technique of creating a design by cutting a shape from one fabric and stitching it to a contrasting fabric backing.

When applying one fabric to another, you can use a matching thread or a contrasting one to define the appliquéd shapes. Pin or baste the shapes in place on the fabric background. You can use an invisible hemming stitch or overcast the raw edges with embroidery floss. If you pin a small section, sew, and then repin another section, the appliqué will be smooth when finished. Check the back to be sure it isn't bunching as you sew.

Machine appliqué is faster than doing it by hand. Mark the fabric with the template. When cutting, leave a seam allowance of ¼ or ½ inch. Pin the appliqué piece to the right side of the background fabric and stitch around the marked stitch line. Cut away the excess fabric as close to the stitch line as possible.

Use a narrow, short zigzag stitch all around the appliqué, covering the straight stitching line.

When appliquéing a pointed piece, narrow the zigzag just before reaching the point on each side.

Fusible webbing such as Stacy's Stitch Witchery is used to fuse appliqués to the background with a hot iron. Sometimes this is enough to hold the appliqué in place for a quick, easy, no-sew project. However, if the item is to be washed—as with a tablecloth, for example—you will want to stitch the edges to secure the appliqué. However, when making fabric collages like the ones on pages 148 and 151, the fusible webbing allows you to work conveniently with small pieces of fabric that do not need sewing.

Oversize pillows

It's quick and easy to make these dramatic, oversize pillows with large, bold blossoms. Very little sewing is involved because you fuse the petals to the muslin background with fusible webbing. Then add details with embroidery floss, markers, or machine stitching. Choose from lively Iris, Pansy, Sunflower, or Periwinkle for a springtime look in any room. The finished pillows are 18 x 18 inches and can be used as floor cushions as well.

Materials (per pillow): Cardboard or tracing paper; colored polyester/cotton blend for flowers and leaves; 2 pieces of muslin 20 x 20 inches; fusible webbing; 1½ pounds polyfil stuffing; waterproof markers (optional).

Directions

Begin tracing each appliqué design (see page 14). Make a pattern of each piece from cardboard or tracing paper. Select the colors to be used for each flower and pin the fabric to fusible webbing. Draw around the corresponding design if using a cardboard template. Or you can pin the tracing paper outline to the fabric and cut out each piece. You will have a double piece (fabric and webbing) for each design element.

Follow the design layout and place each piece of the webbing-backed flower petals on one piece of muslin. Repin these elements here and there to hold in place. Fuse to the muslin with a hot iron. If desired, you can stitch around the leaves and flowers to hold in place. It isn't entirely necessary, but the result will be more permanent. If you have a zigzag attachment on your sewing machine, you can use a very narrow zigzag around the edges.

Use waterproof markers to add details or use contrasting embroidery floss to do this by hand.

Place the second piece of muslin over the front finished piece and stitch around 3 sides and corners, leaving enough fabric open for turning. Trim seams and clip corners. Turn right side out. Press on the wrong side, with flowers face down, on a padded ironing board. Fill with polyfil until the pillow is well packed. Stitch the opening closed with a whipstitch.

Sunflower pillow

Periwinkle pillow

Pansy pillow

Sunflower pillow

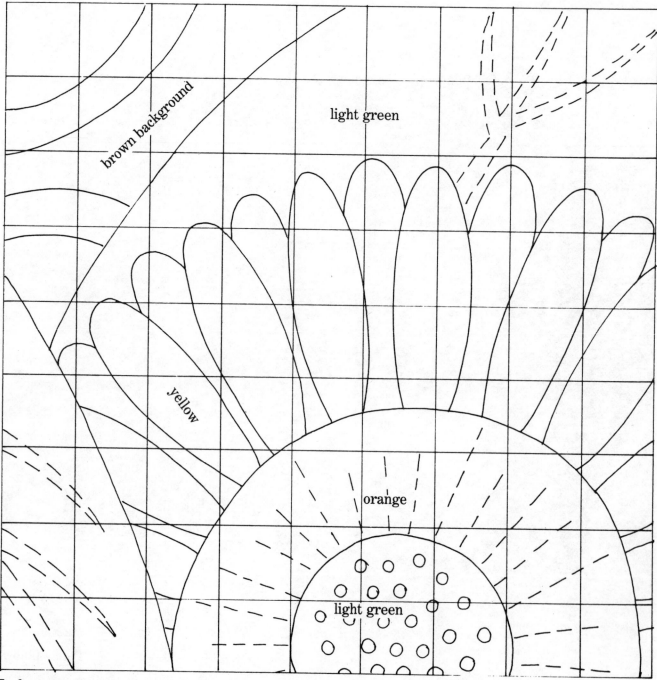

brown background

light green

yellow

orange

light green

Left upper quarter

This pattern as drawn will make a 14 × 14″ pillow. Enlarge pattern for 20 × 20″ pillow. Each square equals 1″.

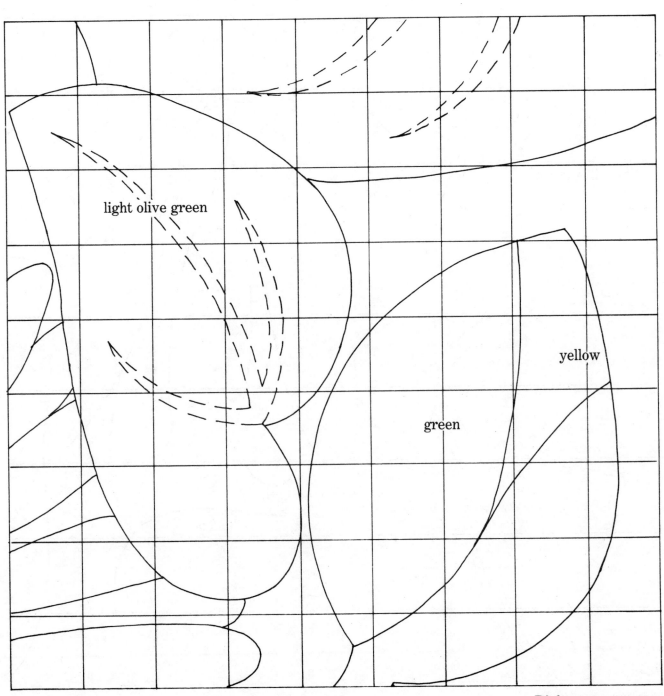

light olive green

yellow

green

Right upper quarter

25

Sunflower pillow

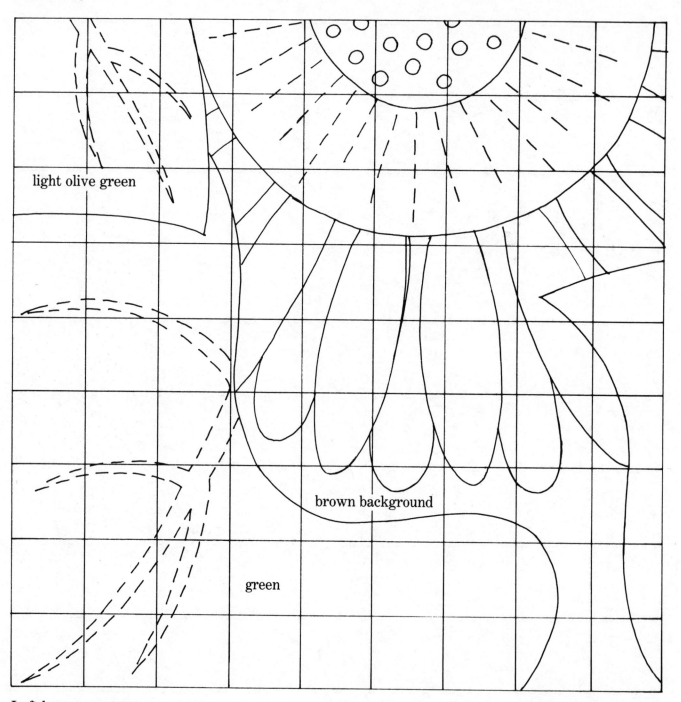

light olive green

brown background

green

Left lower quarter

Each square equals 1″.

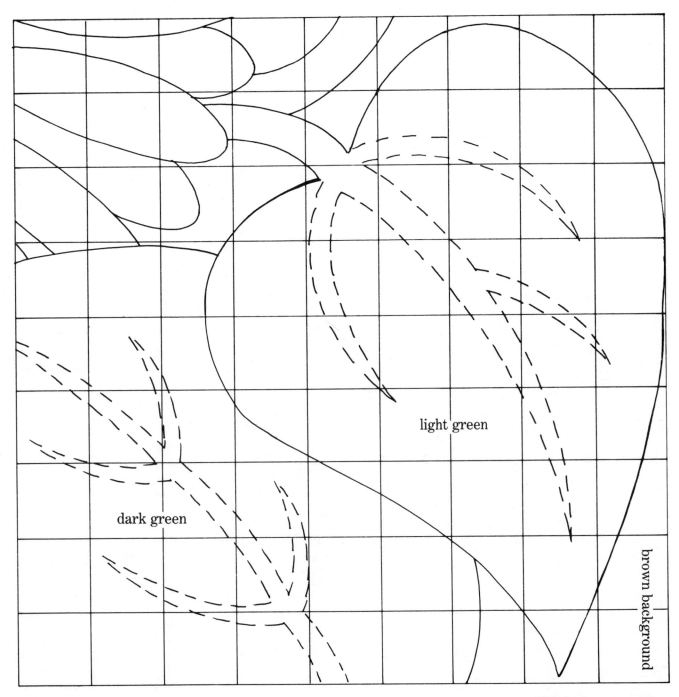

light green

dark green

brown background

Right lower quarter

27

Periwinkle pillow

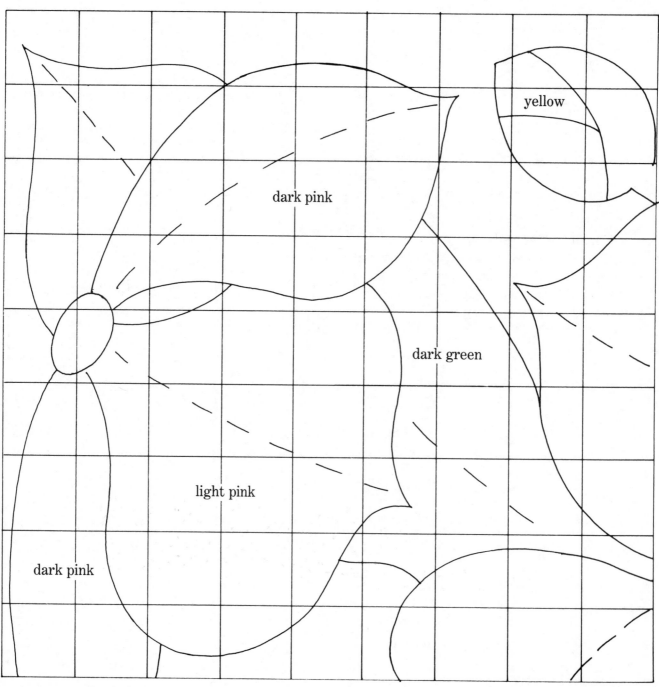

yellow

dark pink

dark green

light pink

dark pink

Left upper quarter

Each square equals 1″.

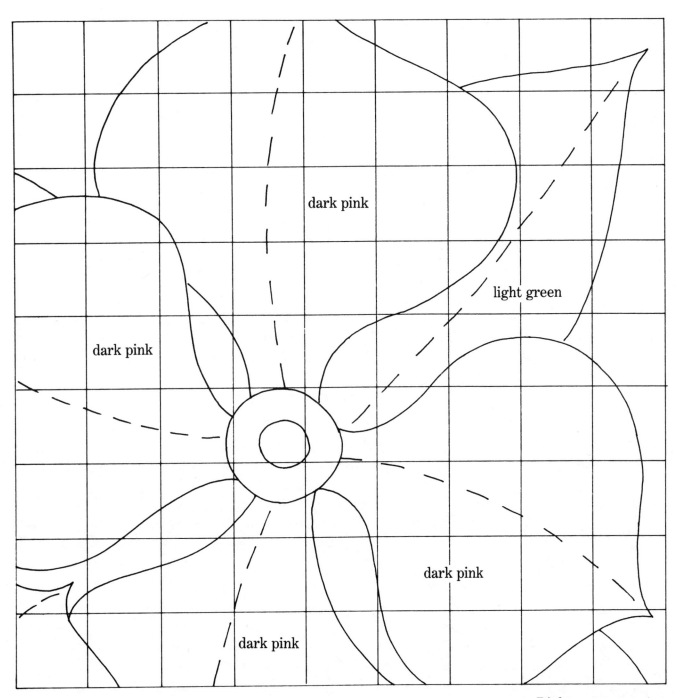

dark pink

light green

dark pink

dark pink

dark pink

Right upper quarter

29

Periwinkle pillow

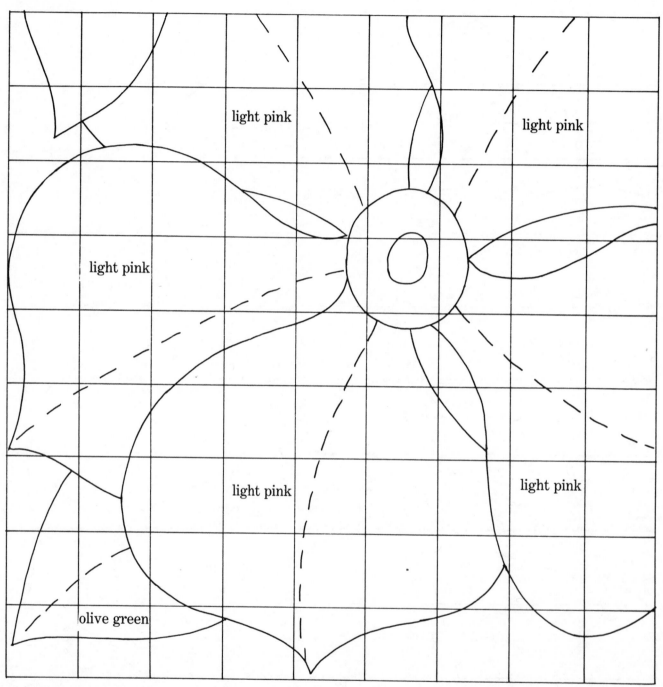

light pink

light pink

light pink

light pink

light pink

olive green

Left lower quarter

Each square equals 1″.

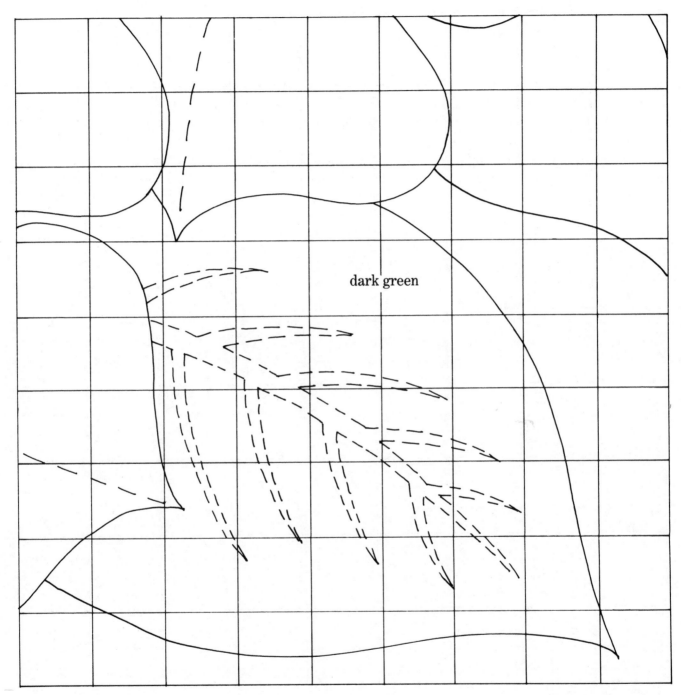

dark green

Right lower quarter

Pansy pillow

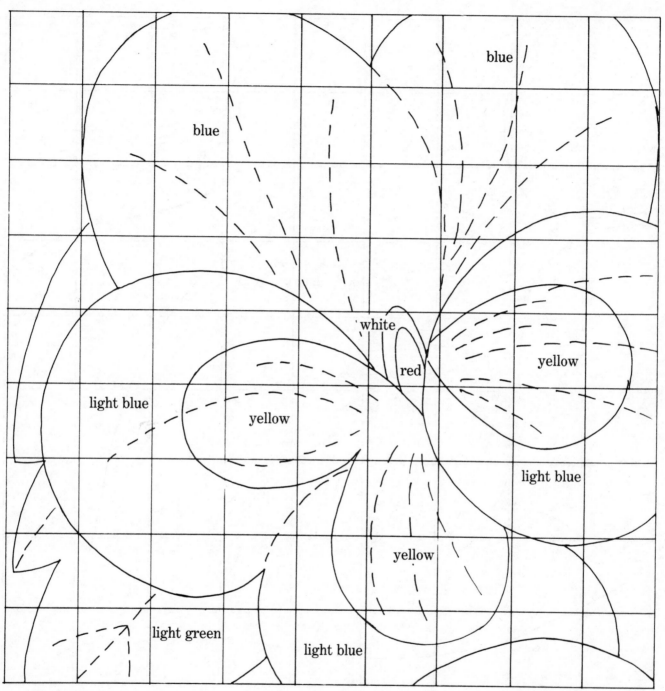

Left upper quarter

Each square equals 1″.

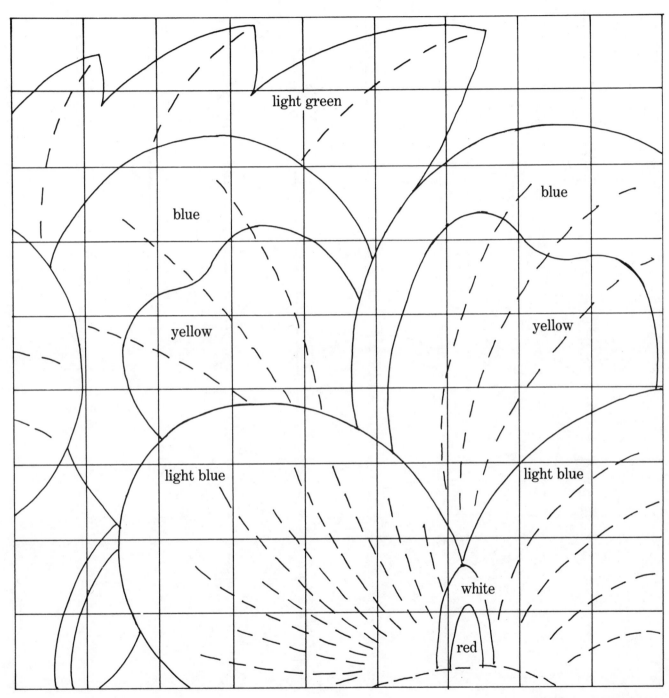

light green

blue

blue

yellow

yellow

light blue

light blue

white

red

Right upper quarter

33

Pansy pillow

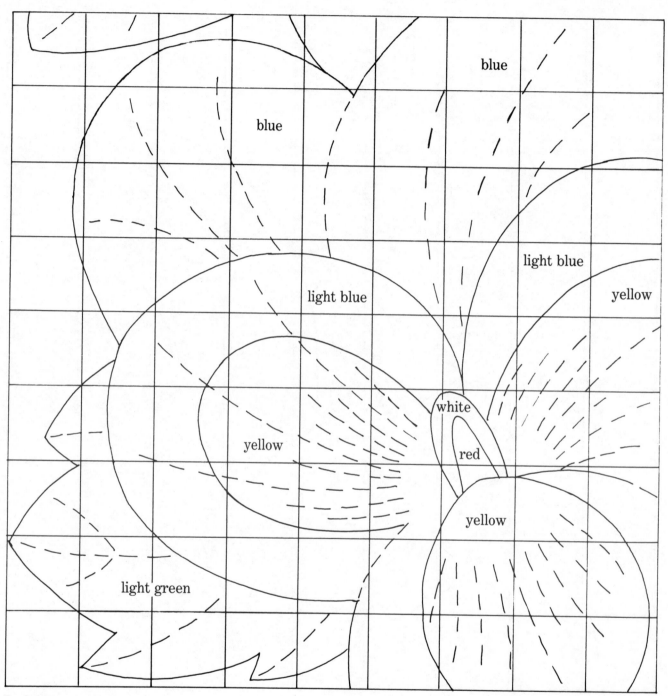

Left lower quarter   Each square equals 1″.

light blue

light green

Right lower quarter

Iris wall hanging

Any of the flower designs can be used as a wall hanging; they will all fit in the same size frame. Directions are given for making the Iris, which is shown matted and framed.

Materials: 2 pieces of muslin 20 x 20 inches; colored cotton or polyester for the appliqués (see pattern for colors); fusible webbing; green matting 25 x 25 inches; frame 29 x 29 inches; cardboard backing 29 x 29 inches.

Directions

Follow the same directions as for making the pillow front on page 20. Place the appliquéd muslin over the cardboard backing and tape to the back to hold in place. Lay matting over the design so the flower fills the entire area. Add the frame and hang.

Iris wall hanging

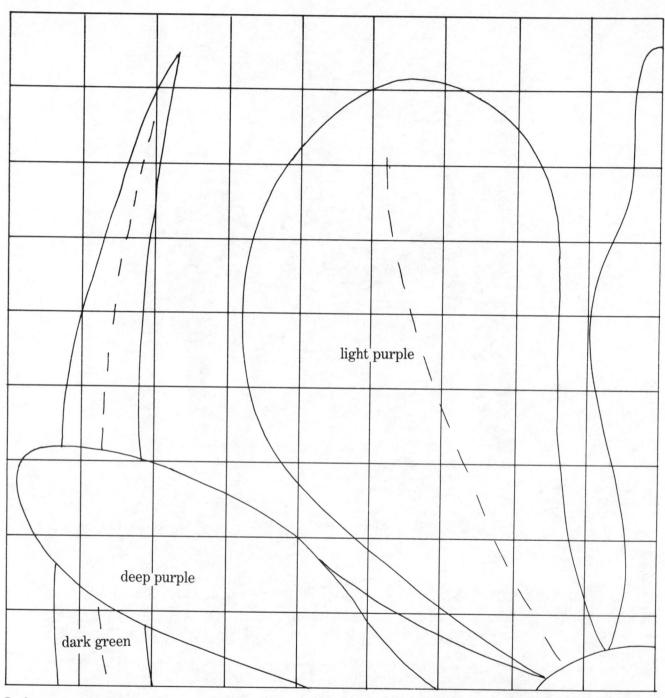

light purple

deep purple

dark green

Left upper quarter

Each square equals 1″.

38

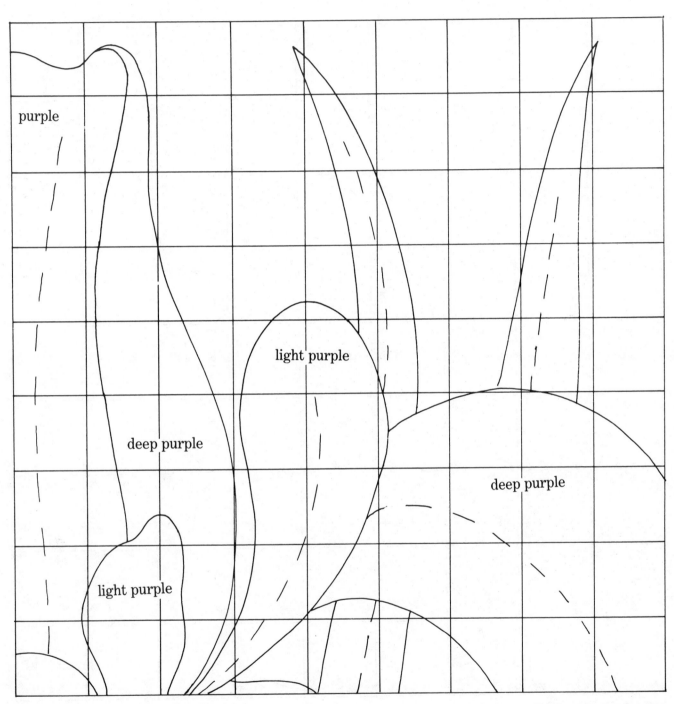

purple

light purple

deep purple

deep purple

light purple

Right upper quarter

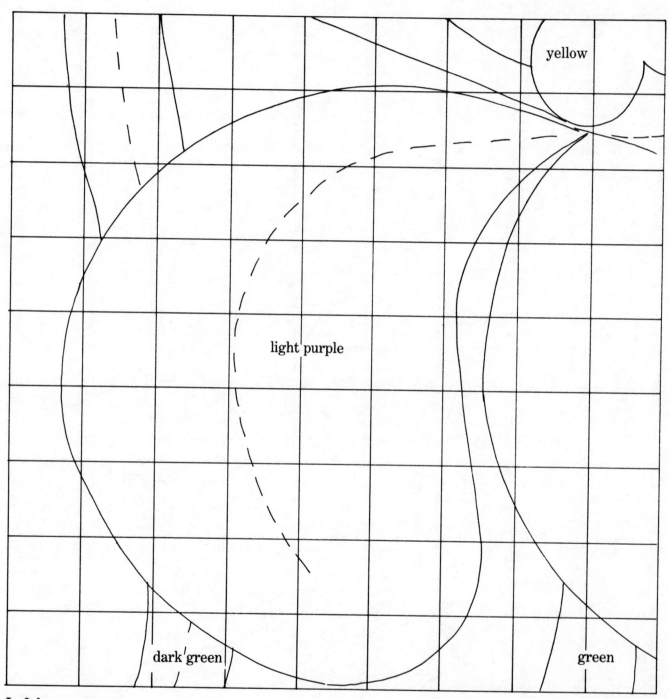

yellow

light purple

dark green

green

Left lower quarter

Each square equals 1″.

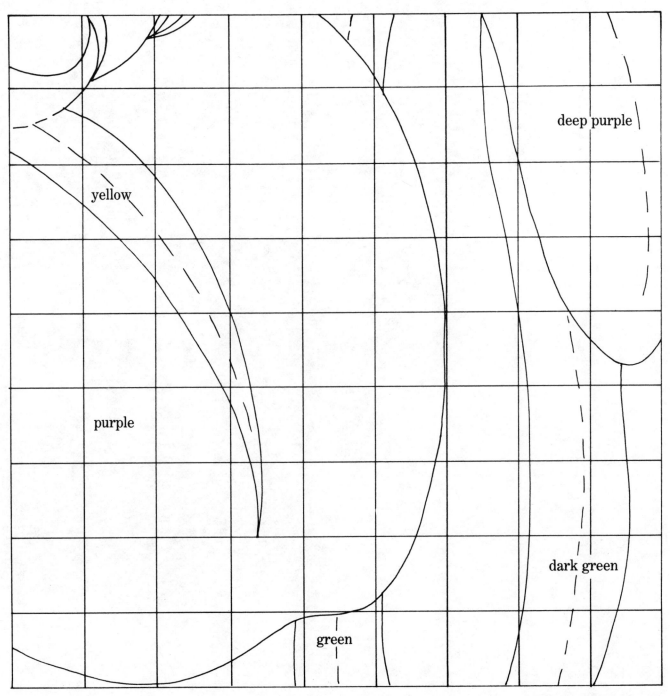

yellow

deep purple

purple

dark green

green

Right lower quarter

Bench cushion

Add a dramatic effect to any bench or chair with a row of tulips growing in the horizon. The number of appliqués you make is determined by the size of your seat area. This design can be easily adjusted and can even be used for back pillows. It's a dramatic way to use all the solid bright-colored cottons in your scrap basket.

The filling will make the finished seat approximately 2 inches high, and the design will extend from the top to the front and slightly under the cushion so it looks continuous.

Materials: 2 pieces of muslin measuring 2 inches wider and 2 inches longer than your seat; a variety of cotton or polyester fabric in green, red, yellow, and brown colors for the appliqués; fusible webbing; 3 pounds polyfil stuffing; waterproof markers (optional).

Directions

Enlarge the design elements (see page 14) and pin the traced patterns to the corresponding colored fabrics together with the fusible webbing. Cut out each pattern piece.

Place the muslin top piece on a flat surface and draw a rectangle to indicate the actual size of your seat. Pin the brown "horizon" piece of fabric and webbing to the bottom portion of the rectangle so it covers the bottom pencil line. Fuse to the muslin with a hot iron.

Next apply green leaves and stems, and tulips in the same way so they are arranged in a row. See the diagram for placement and adjust for your seat size. Add details with waterproof markers if desired.

Place the second piece of muslin over the appliqués and pin along the long edges and across one short end. Stitch together, leaving ¼-inch seam allowance.

Turn right side out and press. Fill with stuffing so that the seat is well padded. Turn the raw edge inside and stitch closed. You might want to attach muslin tie strips to the underside of each corner to keep the cushion from slipping when in use.

Repeat pattern to achieve desired length.

Each square equals 1″.

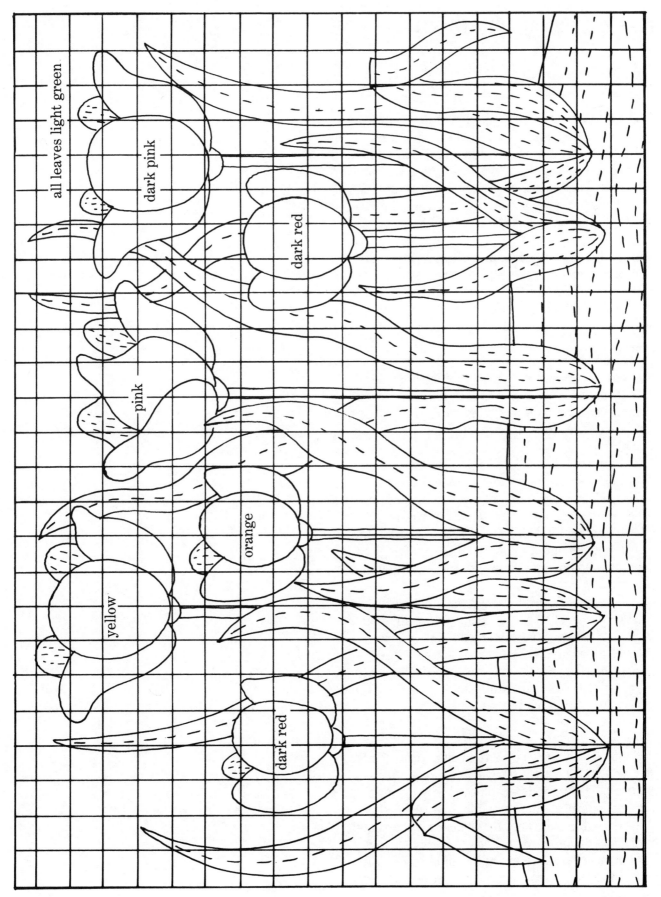

all leaves light green.

dark pink

dark red

pink

orange

yellow

dark red

45

Iris-covered headboard

This headboard is made to fit a double or queen-size bed and is 61 inches wide and 30 inches high. The muslin cover and iris appliqués are padded and quilted, with the ruffle and padded border added on. This design can be made in any colors to match your quilt or coverlet, or use the appliqués on pillows or as a wall hanging.

Materials: Plywood 48 x 61 inches; 2 yards of 60-inch-wide muslin; a pencil; scrap pieces of green, yellow, purple, and lavender cotton; fusible webbing; quilt batting and fiberfil stuffing; stapler; cardboard; glue; masking tape.

Directions

From the plywood, cut a 48-inch-high headboard (measuring from the floor). The width should be the same as your bed frame. Cut curves at the top corners so they are nicely rounded.

Cut a piece of muslin 34 x 60 inches. Measure up 3 inches from the bottom edge and draw a line across. Enlarge each design element (see page 14) and pin each pattern piece to a corresponding colored fabric. Pin this to the fusible webbing and cut each piece out. Follow the diagram for placement of each flower and fuse to the muslin with a hot iron.

Cut a piece of quilt batting the same size as the muslin and baste to the back of the appliquéd front. Quilt each flower and leaves with machine stitches all around the outline of each.

Position the appliquéd muslin on the headboard and staple around all the edges. Trim the top corners to match the plywood.

Border

Using cardboard, cut a template to form a 3-inch-wide border to fit between points A and B on drawing. This template can be made in pieces and stapled together, since it will not show.

Spread glue over the top of the cardboard and press the stuffing over it so you have a puffy border piece. Cut a strip of muslin 4 inches wide and long enough to cover the cardboard strip.

Iris-covered headboard

light purple

purple

yellow

light purple

48   all leaves light green   Repeat pattern to achieve desired length.   Each square equals 1".

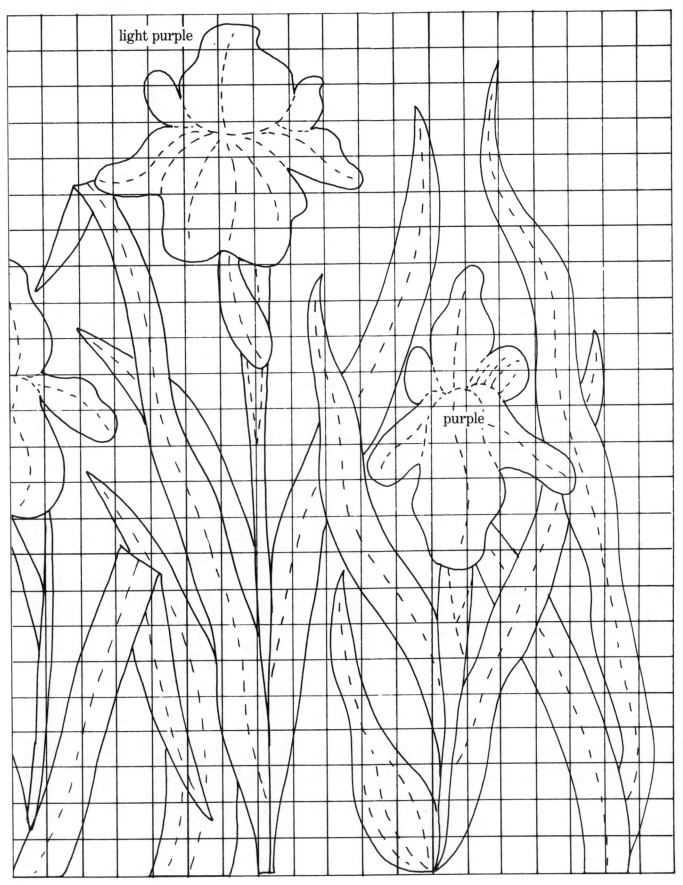

light purple

purple

49

This does not have to be one continuous strip of muslin, since the fabric is crimped as you apply it.

Wrap the muslin over the stuffing, crimping as you do this, and attach the raw edges to the underside with tape. This will create a separate piece to cover the raw edges of the stapled muslin on the headboard.

Ruffle

Piece together strips of muslin 6 inches wide to create one long strip approximately twice the perimeter of the headboard (about 240 inches). Stitch a ¼-inch hem at one edge and both ends.

Divide the muslin ruffle in half and mark with a pin. Divide each half in half again and mark. With right sides up, staple the ruffle at the center mark over the top center edge of the headboard. Next secure each corner where you have marked the muslin. Staple in between, crimping and stapling between these points for an evenly distributed ruffled edge.

Finishing

Spread a thin line of glue around the headboard where the ruffle and muslin have been stapled. Place the crimped border around the headboard, covering the raw edges of the ruffle. Set the headboard against the wall behind the bed or attach it to the bed frame.

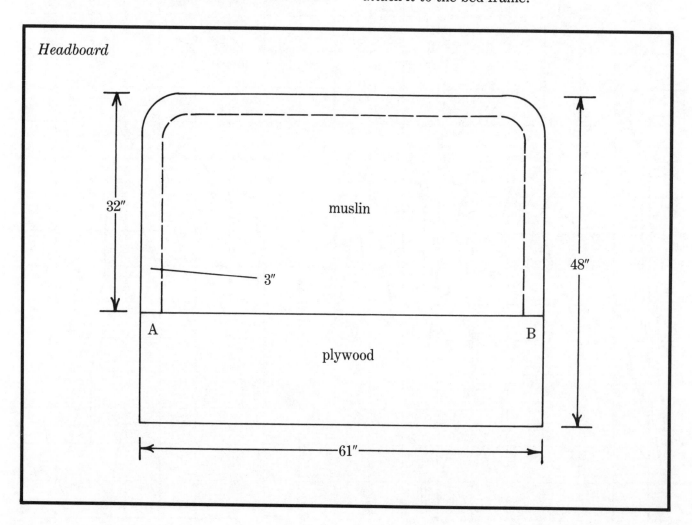

Headboard

Farm scene crib quilt

Make a bright, cheerful quilt for a baby's crib or to fit a youth bed. This lively farm scene is created with scraps of fabric sewn together, over which all the details are appliquéd. Choose the colors that appeal to you and combine solids and prints. Here I've used green calico, blue sky, and brown ground with a calico border. The finished size is 35 x 42 inches but you can adjust the fit by taking away from or adding to the borders.

Materials: A variety of scraps of fabric; fusible webbing: 2 strips of calico for the border 4½ x 45 inches long and 2 strips 4½ x 63½ inches long; a pencil; tracing paper; quilt batting; a piece of muslin for backing fabric 45 x 63 inches.

Directions

Enlarge each pattern piece as per directions on page 14. Pin the background pattern pieces to corresponding fabric and cut out each section. Next pin the appliqué pieces (goose, barn, bow tie, etc.) to the fabric with fusible webbing between and cut out each piece. Do this as well with all the details, such as the barn trim.

With the right sides facing and leaving a ¼-inch seam allowance stitch the background strips together as indicated on the diagram. Open the seams and press.

Pin all the appliqué pieces, such as the barn and goose, to the background as shown. Using a hot iron, fuse the appliqués to the background. Repeat this procedure with all the details, such as the bow around the goose's neck, the trim on the barn, and so on.

With the right sides facing pin the top and bottom border strips to the quilt front and stitch together with ¼-inch seam allowance. Open and press. Attach the long side strips in the same way.

Cut the quilt batting slightly smaller than the quilt size so that the batting does not extend into the seams when the backing is joined to the top. Pin or baste the batting to the back of the quilt top. Straight stitch or zigzag stitch around each appliqué element. Stitch along all seam lines of the design. Quilt along the border seams as well.

To finish

Place the backing fabric face down on the quilt top. Stitch around 3 sides and 4 corners, leaving an opening for turning. Turn the quilt right side out and slipstitch the opening closed.

Add 4″ border all around.

Each square equals 1″.

Country scenes

You will find a variety of wooden embroidery hoops. This makes it possible to work on a quilted appliqué project and hang it as is when finished. The hoop becomes the frame.

Gather a variety of your smallest scraps to create a grouping of different-sized wall hangings. The work can be carried with you and done by hand, and the results are terrific.

Materials: A pencil, tracing paper, and thin cardboard; a variety of fabric scraps; a 12-inch embroidery hoop; quilt batting; a sharp needle; cotton or polyester thread.

Directions

Trace the pattern pieces onto tracing paper and transfer to thin cardboard. Cut out to use as your templates for the appliqué pieces.

When laying out patterns on the fabric, position them so the straight grain of the fabric runs the same direction on both the appliqué and the background fabric. This will keep the fabric from puckering.

Place the fabric face up and draw around the template. This represents the stitch line, not the cutting line. Cut out the pattern pieces 1/4 inch beyond the drawn line.

With the templates on the wrong side of the fabric, turn all edges over the template edges and iron down. Remove the templates and press again. Turn the appliqués right side up and press again.

Place the background fabric in the embroidery hoop. Pin each appliqué piece in position according to the diagram. Whipstitch around all edges of each appliqué piece in the following way:

Bring the needle up through the appliqué about 1/8 inch from the edge and insert it into the background fabric as close as possible to the appliqué edge, making a diagonal stitch. Continue to do this all around.

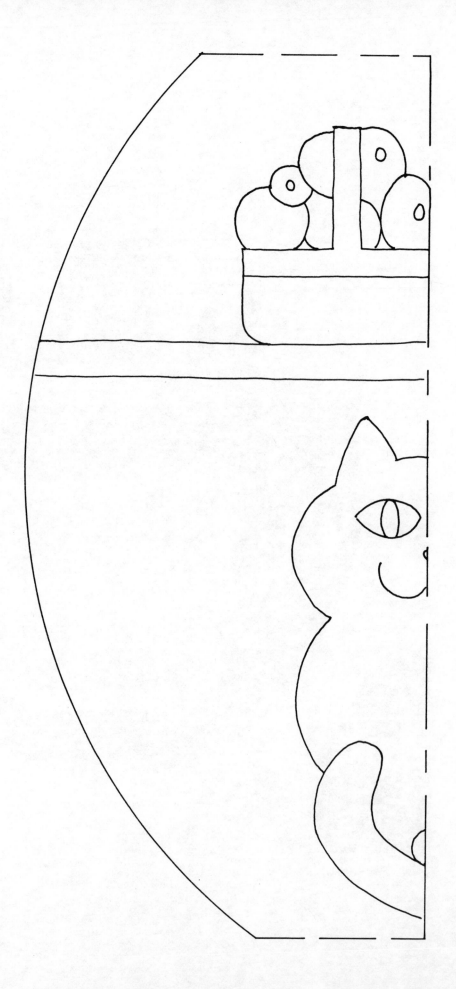

Quilting

If you would like your appliquéd scene to be quilted do so in the following way: Before inserting the background fabric into the embroidery hoop, cut a piece of quilt batting the same size as the inside diameter of the hoop.

Baste the batting to the back of the fabric in a sunburst pattern, starting from the center and working to the outer edges.

Snap the fabric into the hoop and proceed with the appliqués as before. When appliqué stitching is complete, remove basting stitches. For more dimension, add stuffing as for trapunto (see projects on pages 84 and 116) to each appliqué element. For details, add embroidery where desired.

To finish

When all stitching is complete, trim away all excess fabric around the embroidery hoop as close as possible, so that no fabric shows beyond the frame.

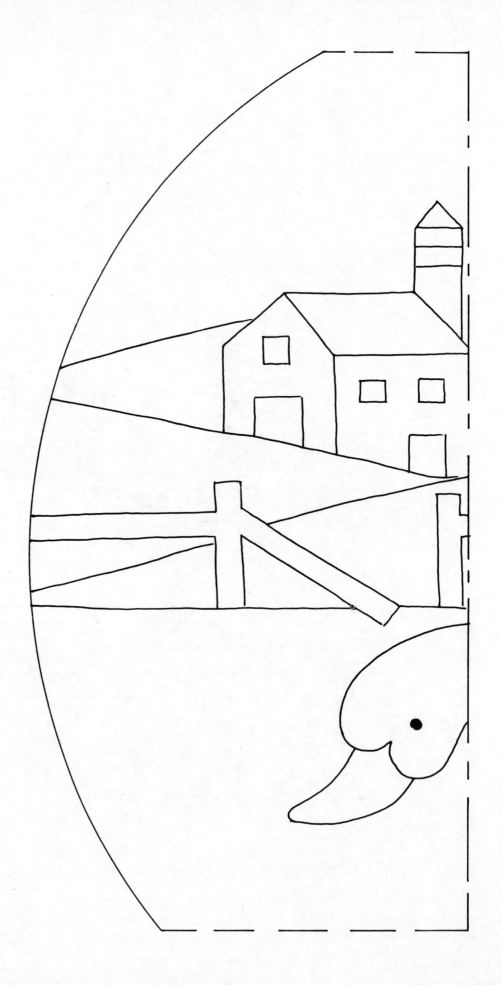

Patchwork is the sewing together of fabric pieces to create an entire design. Sometimes the shapes form a geometric block. The blocks are then sewn together to make up the completed item.

This chapter presents a variety of patchwork projects. The wool coverlet on page 64 is an example of straight-seam sewing of large blocks of fabric to create an overall pattern of different colors and textures. The table runner on page 67 is an example of how you can combine small triangles to form two-patterned squares, which, when joined, make an overall fabric that is multicolored and patterned. It is best to combine materials of the same weight.

Patchwork can be done with irregular pieces of fabric or patches that are all the same size. There are so many variations that one can create it's no wonder that this form of sewing was, and still is, the most popular in our country. Early patchwork quilts are among the most prized, a tradition present-day sewers continue to foster.

Wool coverlet and pillow

Gather all your odds and ends of wool, gabardine, felt, corduroy, and suiting material to make a warm, handsome coverlet. This is a good way to cut up and reuse frayed or worn-out flannel shirts, plaid skirts, and old blankets. Patterns and solids work well together, and if you don't have enough variety on hand, this is a project for which you might want to buy a few ½-yard pieces.

The back is made of 3 strips of remnant wools (or you can use a solid piece) and the border is made from strips of felt. The finished blanket is 48 x 64 inches.

Materials: Remnants of wool fabric; remnants of felt; 15 inch pillow form or polyfil stuffing.

Directions

Cut out a variety of 6-inch squares. For this coverlet you will need 108 to make up the 12 horizontal rows of 9 squares each. Rearrange the squares until you have a nice layout.

With right sides facing and edges aligned, stitch 2 patches together along one edge. Open and press from the wrong side with a steam iron. Continue to do this until you have the desired number of rows.

Place one row right side down over the right side of another and stitch along the edge. Open and press. Continue to attach all rows, taking care to keep the seams aligned as closely as possible.

Piece strips of fabric together to create a backing piece (or use one solid piece of wool fabric) 48 x 64 inches. With wrong sides facing, stitch front and back together with a ½-inch seam allowance.

To make borders

If you use felt for the borders, no hemming will be necessary, as the edges do not fray. Cut 2 strips of felt 4 x 48 inches. Cut 2 strips 4 x 64 inches. These strips can be pieced together if you don't have long enough remnants.

Pin one edge of one short strip to one short end of the front of the cover and stitch ½ inch from

Fruit pillows p. 123

Colorful mirror frame p. 73

Christmas place mat p. 77

Delectable mountain tablecloth p. 136

Country table runner p. 67

Wool coverlet and pillow p. 64

Flowering plant pedestals p. 144

Accent pillows p. 116

Flower pillows p. 92

Ruffled pillow p. 70

Country place mat p. 79

Iris wall hanging p. 36

Heart hanging p. 86

Oversize pillows p. 20

Iris-covered headboard p. 46

Bench cushion p. 43

Animal pillows p. 128

Log cabin quilt p. 112

Four flowers pillow p. 107

Apple picture p. 148

Floor cushion p. 94

Crib quilt p. 89

Basket full of strawberries p. 139

Star pillow p. 105

Summer collage p. 151

Farm scene crib quilt p. 51

Country scenes p. 54

Wool coverlet and pillow

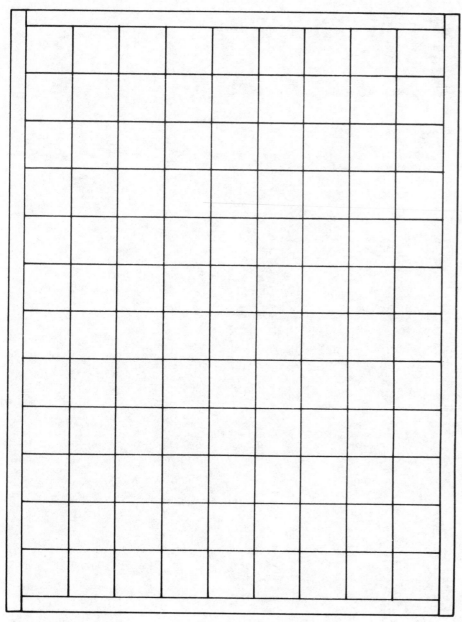

Assembly diagram

the raw edges. Turn the border to the wrong side and stitch as for the front. Repeat on the long edges with the remaining border strips.

Pillow

Stitch together 3 rows of 3 squares each. Cut a backing piece the same size as the front. With right sides facing, stitch around 3 sides and 4 corners. Turn right side out and insert a pillow form or stuff with polyfil. Slipstitch the open edges closed.

Get out all your odds and ends of fabric scraps for this 22 x 64–inch table runner. Made of patchwork triangles, it is a delight to work on. The colors and patterns look good in any combination, and the more colorful the better. The finished runner is then edged with satin blanket binding and braided trim for a smart, finished look.

Materials: A pencil, tracing paper, and thin cardboard; a variety of light and dark cotton scraps; 4 yards each of blanket binding and braid.

Directions

Trace the triangle pattern onto a sheet of tracing paper and transfer to thin cardboard, such as a manilla folder. This is the template from which you will cut the patches, leaving an extra 1/4 inch on all sides for seam allowance. You will need 240 triangles.

When attaching triangles to make up each square, try to combine light and dark colors for an interesting contrast. With right sides facing, seam 2 triangles together along the longest edge. Open to form a square and press on the wrong side. Repeat to make 120 squares.

Arrange the squares into 20 horizontal rows of 6 and move them around until you have a pleasing layout, with alternating light and dark colors next to each other.

With right sides facing, seam squares together to create the rows. Join rows in the same way, taking special care to line up the seams.

Cut one piece (or piece small pieces of fabric together) for the backing. If you prefer, you can leave the back with raw seams and not finish it, but this is an added touch. With wrong sides facing, stitch together 1/4 inch from the edges all around.

Finish the edges with satin blanket binding in a color to match the dominating color in the runner. This can be machine stitched or done by hand with a whipstitch. Attach braid along the inside edge of the binding to finish.

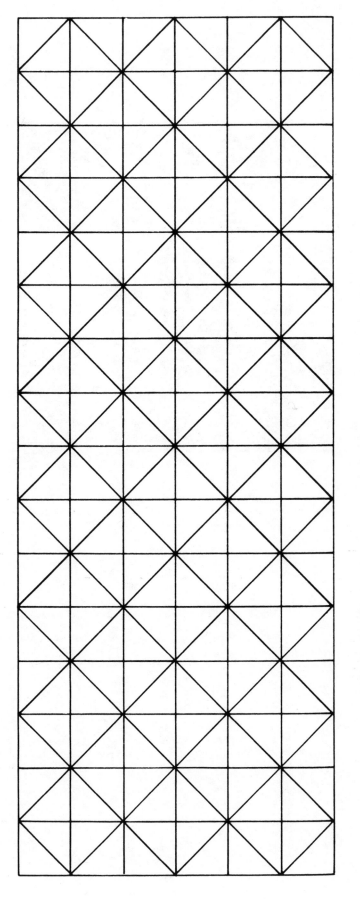

Create a pleasing design of darks and lights when assembling patches.

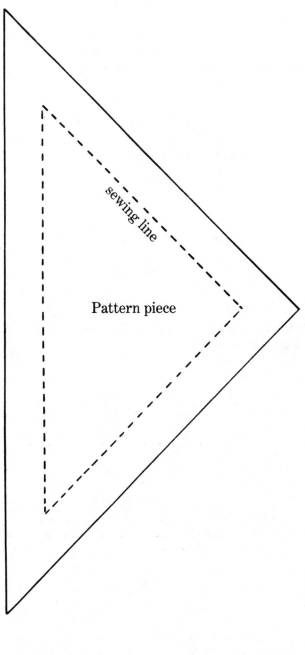

sewing line

Pattern piece

Ruffled pillows

Make a couple of pillows from the same scraps as the table runner on page 67. You can make these as throw pillows, or make them to fit your dining chairs to go with the runner. These are 12 inches square.

Materials (for each pillow): A pencil, tracing paper, and thin cardboard; a variety of light and dark cotton scraps; polyfil stuffing or a 12-inch pillow form.

Directions

Trace the triangle pattern on page 69 onto a sheet of tracing paper and transfer to thin cardboard. When cutting out each triangular shape, allow for a ¼-inch seam allowance all around.

For each pillow, cut 16 light and 16 dark triangles. With right sides facing, seam a light and dark piece together along the longest edge. Open and press the seams on the wrong side.

Seam the squares together into 4 horizontal rows of 4 squares each, with light and dark patches alternating against one another.

Seam one row below the other to complete the pillow top. Cut a solid piece, such as an overall calico print, for the backing.

Cut a 3½ x 96–inch strip of pretty fabric to match one of the fabrics in the patchwork and seam the short ends together. Stitch a ¼-inch hem along one long edge. Divide the loop into 4 equal parts and mark with pins.

With right sides facing, pin the raw edges of the ruffle and pillow top together, gathering the fabric evenly as you do this. The pinned marks should meet at each corner of the pillow top. Machine-stitch ¼ inch from the edges all around.

Place the backing piece right side down over the top piece with the ruffle between and stitch together along the seam line. Leave one side open for turning. Turn right side out and stuff. Turn in the open edges and slipstitch.

Create a variety of pillows by varying the patterns.

Colorful mirror frame

Use colorful strips of fabric to make a padded mirror frame. This one is 14 x 18 inches, but you can make any size frame and have a mirror cut to size at your local hardware store. The mirror area here is 9 x 13 inches.

Materials: A variety of colorful fabric scraps; a 9 x 13 inch mirror; 2 pieces of ⅛-inch Fomecore 14 x 18 inches; a 14 x 18 inch posterboard; glue; a craft knife or razor blade; rubber cement; quilt batting; masking tape; a tab for hanging.

Directions

Cut 40 strips of fabric 1½ x 5½ inches. To make the side borders place one strip face down on top of another and stitch along the 5½-inch edge, leaving a ¼-inch seam allowance. Open and press. Continue to attach strips in this way until you have 12 strips. Repeat. Seam 8 strips together in the same way and make 2 for the top and bottom borders. You will now have 2 patchwork strips 12 inches long and 2 that are 8 inches long.

Seam a 5½-inch square piece to each end of the 8-inch-long pieces. With right sides facing and raw edges matching, attach a 12-inch-long strip to the top of one square. Open and press. Repeat on the opposite side. Attach the last strip to complete the frame.

Center the mirror on the posterboard and draw around the outside edge of the mirror. Cut this with a craft knife and lift out the posterboard center. Glue the posterboard frame, with the mirror set in the center, over one piece of Fomecore. Set aside to dry.

From the second piece of Fomecore cut an opening 8½ x 12½ that will frame the mirror. Glue strips of quilt batting to this Fomecore "frame." Place the fabric frame over the batting and turn the outside raw edges over to the wrong side of the foam frame. Tape the edges down with masking tape. Clip the inside corners to miter them. Next, turn the inside raw edges over to the wrong side of the Fomecore. Tape these edges down so the fabric is taut and smooth on the front. This may require picking up the taped areas and retaping here and there as you work out the wrinkles all around.

Apply rubber cement to the taped back of the fabric frame and to the posterboard around the mounted mirror. Let these pieces dry.

Place the fabric frame over the mirror so that the edges of the mirror are covered by the fabric frame all around. Press down. Attach the tab for hanging to the back.

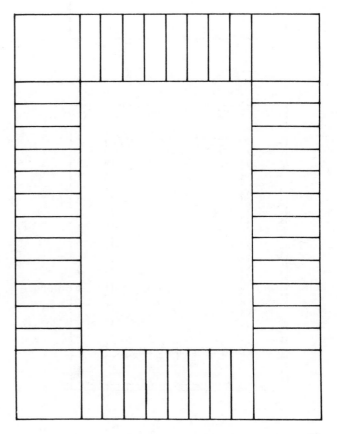

Colorful mirror frame

Padded mirror

1. 14 × 18″ Fomecore backing
2. 14 × 18″ poster board with 9 × 13″ mirror in center
3. 14 × 18″ Fomecore frame with 8½ × 12½″ opening and batting mounted on front
4. Patchwork covering

Mount No. 2. on No. 1. Attach patchwork cover No. 4 to No. 3. Mount unit 3–4 on unit 1–2.

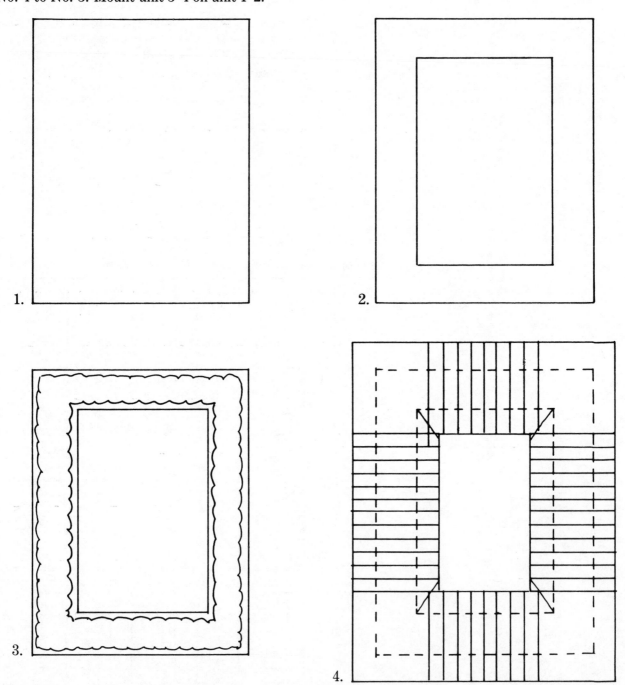

76

Christmas place mat

It's always fun to add a little Christmas spirit to your decorating during the holidays. Make a colorful patchwork place mat from all the red and green scraps you have left over from other projects. This makes a good last-minute gift, or bazaar item. If you use scraps it doesn't have to cost you a cent. The finished size is 12 x 16 inches.

Materials (for 1 place mat): A variety of green and red printed fabric scraps; quilt batting; backing fabric 12 x 16 inches; 1 package 1-inch-wide hem facing.

Directions

Cut all the scrap fabric pieces into 2½-inch squares. This allows for ¼-inch seam allowance.

Arrange so the pieces look best together. With right sides facing, stitch 2 patches together along one edge. Open and press the seam. Continue to join patches until you have 8 rows of 6 squares.

With right sides facing and edges aligned, join the rows so you have 8 across and 6 down. Cut batting the same size as the place mat top and pin top, batting, and backing together. Machine-stitch to quilt along all seam lines.

To finish, stitch the hem facing ¼ inch in from the raw edge all around the top. Fold to the back and stitch to the back edge ¼ inch in from the raw edge. Press.

Country place mat

Make a set of country place mats using pastel colors with an overall small print. Try to select one fabric with a colored background and an overall white print, and another fabric with a white background and a colored print. This will provide contrast of light and dark for the borders.

It's quick and easy to stitch a patchwork border leaving a center area for a pretty, quilted design. A large heart fills the center panel of this project.

Add a border of piping and lace with a bow at each corner for a delightful addition to any breakfast corner. The finished size, including the eyelet, is 12 x 16 inches.

Country place mat

Materials: Scraps of blue and white fabric for the borders; pink printed fabric for the center; a piece of fabric in one of the prints 11½ x 15½ inches for the backing; quilt batting 11 x 15 inches; 2 yards eyelet (includes bows); 1½ yards of welting.

Directions

Cut 10 strips of the light fabric 1½ x 3½ inches. Cut 12 strips of the contrasting fabric 1½ x 3½ inches. Cut a center piece (pink) 9½ x 11½ inches.

With right sides facing and top edges aligned, stitch a light and dark strip (A and B on diagram) together with ¼-inch seam allowance. Open and press. Continue to do this until you have 2 separate border strips of 11 pieces each. Each border should have dark strips top and bottom.

With right sides facing and edges aligned, stitch the borders to each long edge of the center panel. Open and press.

Trace the heart pattern and transfer it to the center of the pink panel (C). Next pin the place mat to the quilt batting. Machine- or hand-stitch along the drawn lines. Quilt in this way along all seam lines of the borders.

With raw edges matching, pin the welting all around on the front of the place mat and stitch together. Attach the eyelet in the same way.

Pin the backing material to the front of the place mat making sure that the eyelet will not get caught in the seam when stitching the back to the front. Stitch around 3 edges and 4 corners. Clip excess fabric around the raw edges. Turn right side out and stitch opening closed. Make eyelet or ribbon bows, if preferred, and stitch to each corner for a pretty finish.

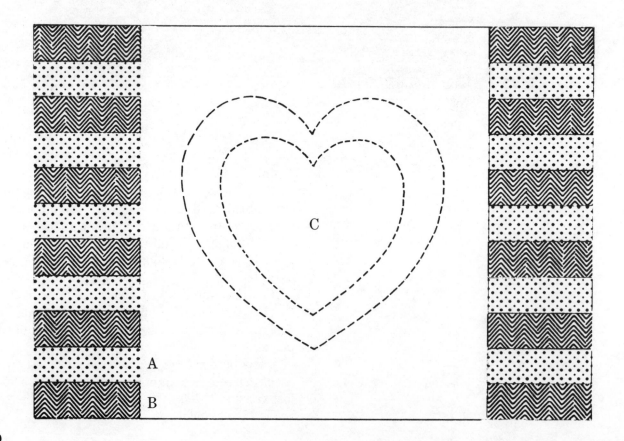

Quilting

Quilting is the means by which you stitch together 2 layers of fabric with a layer of batting between. The lines or markings on fabric that make up the design is a quilting pattern. Small hand or machine stitches are sewn along these lines, which might be straight or curved or made up of elaborately curlicued patterns. These stitches define a design, making it appear almost three-dimensional and giving it a sculptured effect.

The top of a quilt or quilted hanging or pillow is the front layer of fabric with the right side showing. The backing is the bottom layer and is usually made from a lightweight fabric, such as cotton or unbleached muslin.

Hand quilting: The most comfortable way to do your quilting is over a frame or in a hoop. The fabric remains taut, allowing you to make even stitches. It's important to have your fabric and batting basted and marked before quilting each section. When removed from the frame or hoop, your quilting will have a nicely puffed effect.

Machine quilting: This is an easier, quicker method of quilting and creates a much different effect. It is best to do it when the batting isn't too thick.

Trapunto: This is a method for quilting and stuffing to create a puffy or three-dimensional effect in certain areas of the design. The project on page 84 will show you how to do this technique, which can be done on printed fabric for an exciting effect.

Trapunto floral picture

If you have a small piece of fabric with an illustration or overall floral design, it is easy to quilt around the design and frame for hanging.

This might be a good way to coordinate existing pieces in a room. Use leftover curtain or slipcover fabric, or tie the project in with a tablecloth or throw pillows.

The craft of trapunto is the process by which you create a raised or stuffed form of quilting. Each quilted design element is given extra padding to create a three-dimensional effect. In this way flowers, for example, look more real.

Materials: Quilt batting; remnant of floral print; backing piece same size as print; canvas stretchers (available in art stores); staple gun; polyfil stuffing; frame (optional).

Directions

Cut the quilt batting slightly smaller than the printed fabric. Cut backing fabric the same size as the top piece. With wrong sides facing, pin around the edges to secure the front and back pieces with batting between.

Begin at the center of the fabric and machine-stitch around the floral outlines. Continue to work outward until all flowers are quilted.

It is easiest to stretch the quilted fabric over stretchers before doing the trapunto. The stretchers come in all sizes, so measure the finished quilted fabric before going to the art store. You will need approximately 2 inches all around for stapling the fabric to the back of the stretchers. Place the fabric over the frame. Begin at the center of one edge and pull the fabric to the back. Staple in place. Continue to do this in the center of each side edge. Next pull the corners so they are taut and staple to the back. Continue to pull and staple the fabric until it is stretched and secure.

Slit the fabric at the back of each design element and insert polyfil. If you use a blunt instrument such as a crochet hook, you can distribute the stuffing evenly and get it into narrow areas. When complete, you can slipstitch all slash lines closed or leave as is, since the back will be against the wall. The "picture" is now ready for framing, or you can hang as is.

Heart hanging

Create this quilted wall hanging in one evening. Made to resemble the heavily quilted baby coverlets of early American days, the work has been simplified by using fusible webbing for the appliqués. The background is prequilted fabric to avoid tedious stitching. Of course, if you want to quilt each heart it will be that much nicer. Or, consider using a machine zigzag stitch around each appliqué. The finished project is 28 x 28 inches.

Materials: A pencil, tracing paper, and thin cardboard; 1 yard prequilted white fabric; a variety of red scrap fabric; fusible webbing; 2 packages royal blue 2-inch-wide hem facing; Velcro for hanging.

Directions

Use the pattern provided and make a template to the exact size. To do this, trace the heart onto a sheet of tracing paper, then transfer it to thin cardboard and cut out. Either use this heart to trace around or use the cut-out area to draw your heart outline onto the fabric.

Pin each fabric scrap to fusible webbing and cut out each heart. Position the hearts on the quilted background in straight rows of 6 across and 6 down. There should be a border of 2 inches of white fabric all around. Fuse the hearts in position with a hot iron.

Fold the hem facing over the raw edges so you have 1-inch borders on the front and back of the quilted fabric. Pin and stitch all around.

To hang

Stitch a strip of Velcro to the top and bottom back edges of the quilt. Attach corresponding Velcro strips to the wall. Attach the hanging.

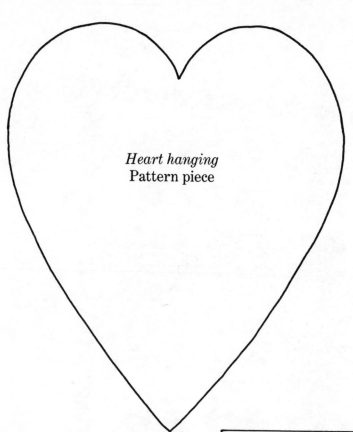

Heart hanging
Pattern piece

Crib quilt

This baby blanket is made from 4 different fabrics, and the finished size is 32 x 40 inches. It has extra padding all around and the center squares are puffy to create a coverlet that is light to sleep under and is soft as a cloud for baby to sit on.

This is a good portable project because the center is made of individually sewn squares that are then stuffed and stitched together.

Materials: ⅝ yard each of pink and white print for the patches; ¾ yard of muslin; ⅜ yard of blue print; 2 yards of pink for backing and border; polyfil stuffing for center patches; quilt batting for the borders.

Directions

Cut the following pieces of fabric. The number of pieces to be cut from each appear in parentheses.

Fabric A (pink) 6-inch squares (18)
Fabric B (white) 6-inch squares (17)
Muslin 5-inch squares (35)
Fabric C (blue) border strips 5½ x 21 inches (2)
Fabric C (blue) border strips 5½ x 39 inches (2)
Fabric D (pink) backing piece 38 x 46 inches (1)
Quilt batting strips 7 x 34 inches (2)
Quilt batting strips 7 x 42 inches (2)

Center patches

Pin each 6-inch patch (A and B) to a 5-inch muslin piece with right sides out and corners matching. Fold the extra fabric into a tuck at the center of each edge. Stitch around 3 sides and 4 corners, leaving the center of the fourth edge open for stuffing. Stuff each pocket.

Begin with a pink patch and a white patch and, with a ¼-seam allowance, stitch together along the open edges with right sides facing. If it is difficult to maneuver the stuffed patches, use a zipper foot on your machine.

Continue to stitch rows of 5 patches together, alternating colors A and B, until you have 7 rows of 5 patches each. With right sides facing join all rows.

90

Borders

With right sides facing, seam the short border pieces (C) to the short ends of the patchwork center. Repeat on the sides with the longer border pieces (C).

Place the quilt top in the center of the quilt backing with wrong sides together. There will be approximately 4 inches of the backing extending beyond the top edges all around. Pin together and stitch along the inside border seams through both layers.

Place the strips of batting under the top borders. There will be 2 inches of batting extended beyond border edges all around.

Binding

Turn the quilt backing edges under ½ inch to the wrong side and press. Fold this edge over to the right side and pin the turned-under edge to the top of the blue (C) border. Stitch along this seam line through batting and backing to finish.

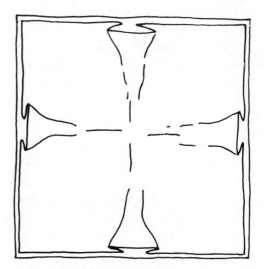

Sew three sides and stuff.

Flower pillows

It's easy to quilt any floral print. You can duplicate this project for under $10.00. All it takes is one yard of VIP "Manor House" fabric. There are six different flowers framed within borders per yard. Once quilted, the fabric is used to make these handsome pillows that are 14 x16 inches.

Materials: 1 yard VIP fabric; ½ yard solid fabric for backing; quilt batting; 62 inches of welting; hem facing to cover cording (or use leftover fabric); polyfil stuffing (8 ounces per pillow).

Directions

Cut the rectangular panels for each pillow, leaving ¼-inch seam allowance. For other fabric, cut 2 pieces 14½ x 16½ inches.

Cut quilt batting slightly smaller than the fabric and pin this to the back of the flowered fabric panel.

Begin at the center of the fabric and machine-stitch around the floral outline. Continue to work outward until all the flowers are quilted. If the fabric has borders, as this does, quilt along these lines as well.

With raw edges aligned and welting toward the center of the pillow front, pin the welting all around. With right sides facing, stitch backing and front together around 3 sides and 4 corners. Turn right side out and stuff. Slipstitch the open edges closed.

Floor cushion

This floor cushion is 24 inches square and made from scraps of blue calico and muslin. It has a pretty quilted design in the borders that can be worked by hand or machine. Consider making 3 pillows to line the back of a day bed. This was designed and made by my daughter Robby.

Materials: ½ yard blue printed fabric; ¾ yard 45-inch-wide muslin; quilt batting; compass and pencil; ruler; polyfil stuffing.

Directions

Cut the following pieces of fabric. The numbers in parentheses indicate how many of each.

Blue fabric: 12½-inch square (1)
              2½-inch squares (20)
              2½ x 12½–inch strips (4)
Muslin: 2½ x 12–inch strips (8)
              2½-inch squares (16)
              24½-inch square for backing (1)

To make 9-patch blocks

With right sides facing, seam one 2½-inch muslin square between two 2½-inch blue squares. Repeat. Next seam 1 blue square between 2 muslin squares. Seam the 3 rows, one below the other with a blue square in the middle. Make 3 more blocks the same way. These represent each corner piece.

Seam a blue strip between 2 muslin strips. Repeat 3 times. With right sides facing, stitch the row assembly to opposite sides of the large blue square.

With right sides facing, stitch a 9-patch block at each short end of the 2 remaining row assemblies. With right sides facing and edges aligned, stitch these pieces to the top and bottom of the central assembly. This completes the pillow top assembly.

Quilting

Cut a piece of quilt batting the same size as the pillow front and pin to the back. With a compass and a light pencil, draw overlapping 5-inch circles in the center square on front side of pillow (see diagram). Rule diagonal lines across the borders with ½-inch spaces between. Sew running stitches along the drawn lines to quilt.

To finish

With right sides facing, pin top and backing together. Stitch around 3 sides and 4 corners with ¼-inch seam allowance. Turn right side out and stuff. Turn in the open edges and slipstitch.

Piecing diagram

Floor cushion

Quilting pattern

Peony wall hanging

You can make this red, white, and blue wall hanging as a decorative piece or as a quilt. The finished size is 54 x 54 inches square, but if you add more rows you can increase the size for your bed measurement. Since this project is intended as a hanging, I used fusible webbing to make the appliqués rather than turning edges in the traditional manner used for bed quilts. This makes it easy to complete this project in a weekend.

Materials: (All fabric 45 inches wide) 1 yard white cotton fabric; 1 yard blue cotton fabric; 1½ yards red cotton fabric; 1 yard dark blue fabric; fusible webbing; 1½ yards quilt batting; 1½ yards muslin or backing material; 3 packages of 2-inch-wide royal blue hem facing or a piece of dark blue fabric (can be pieced) 10 x 59 inches for the border strips; Velcro for hanging.

Directions

Cut 18 white squares 8½ x 8½ inches. Cut 18 light blue squares 8½ x 8½ inches.

Trace petal pattern piece (A). Transfer to cardboard and cut out the template (see page 16). Cut out 18 pieces from red fabric.

Trace the stem and leaf piece (B) and make template as for pattern A. Pin the dark blue fabric to fusible webbing, and cut out 18 pattern pieces.

Place each flower top (A) over fusible webbing, pin together, and cut out. Follow the diagram and position a stem and leaf with fusible webbing on each 8½-inch white square. Fuse with a hot iron. Repeat with the flower.

Beginning with a white square, and with right sides facing and edges aligned, join blue and white squares alternating to make 6 rows of 6. Join the rows in the same way.

Cut quilt batting and backing fabric the same size as the quilt top. Place the batting between top and backing and stitch together along the seam lines between squares. To quilt the designs, stitch around edges of flowers, stems, and leaves.

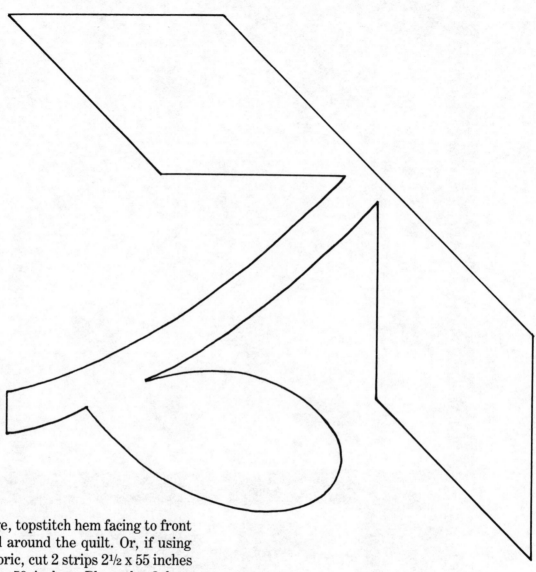

To finish the edge, topstitch hem facing to front and back edges all around the quilt. Or, if using extra dark blue fabric, cut 2 strips 2½ x 55 inches and 2 strips 2½ x 59 inches. Place the 2 long strips face down on each side edge of the quilt and stitch with a ¼-inch seam allowance. Stitch the remaining strips to the top and bottom edge of the quilt. Fold the raw edges under ¼ inch and stitch to the back edge of the quilt. Slipstitch where the border overlaps at each corner.

To hang

Attach a strip of Velcro to the top back of quilt. Attach corresponding Velcro piece to the wall and attach the quilt. Pull so hanging is taut and repeat at bottom edge.

Rocking chair cushion

Most rocking chairs are the same size, and it's easy to make a cushion to fit the seat. To make sure that yours will fit exactly, it's important to make a paper pattern that's slightly larger. This is a nice way to coordinate a piece of furniture with the fabrics in the room.

Materials: 1/2 yard cotton fabric (blue background used here); scrap of pink fabric for appliqué; fusible webbing; quilt batting; enough piping to go around cushion; polyfil stuffing.

Directions

Make a pattern of your chair seat and cut 2 pieces of fabric 1 1/2 inches larger all around. Trace the appliqué pattern piece and pin to pink fabric. Cut 8 pieces leaving an extra 1/4 inch all around for seam allowance.

With right sides facing, stitch 2 appliqué pieces together along one edge (see diagram). Continue to do this until you have half a star with 4 points. Repeat for the other half of the star. With right sides facing and long straight edges aligned, stitch top and bottom portion of the star together. Open and press the seams on the back.

Place the 8-point star over fusible webbing and cut out a web piece to match. Pin both layers to the center front of the top cushion piece and fuse with a hot iron.

Cut quilt batting the same size as the top piece and pin to the back of the fabric. Machine-stitch with contrasting thread (blue) along the seamed lines of the star and zigzag if desired around points that are not joined.

With right sides facing, pin the raw edge of the piping between cushion pieces around outer edge. Stitch around the edge, leaving approximately 5 inches open at the back for turning. Clip around the edges to the seam line. Turn to the right side and press.

Fill the cushion with polyfil stuffing and stitch the opening closed. Use scraps of blue fabric to make ties to attach to the back cushion edges to hold it in place on the chair seat.

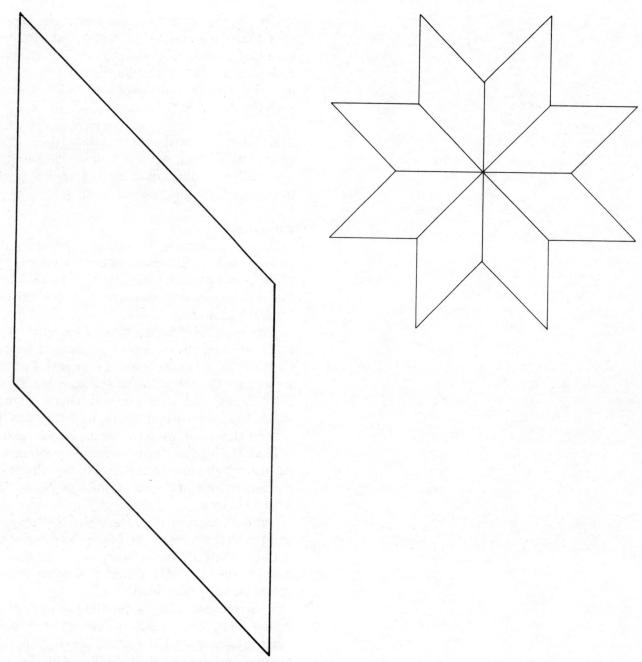

Template for rocking chair seat and star pillow

Early American pillows

Star pillow

The designs for these pillows match the wall hanging on page 98 and will look good on a couch or bed under the quilted hanging. While I used country colors of faded red, blue, and green, you can choose any color or printed fabric to match your room decor. The finished pillows are 16 x 16 inches with the borders and 14 x 14 inches without borders. There is a 2-inch eyelet ruffle around each pillow.

Materials (per pillow): ½ yard white cotton fabric; scraps of red, green, and blue fabric; a pencil, tracing paper, and thin cardboard; 2 yards white eyelet; polyfil stuffing or appropriate size pillow form.

Four flowers pillow

Directions

Cut a white fabric square 14½ x 14½ inches. Cut a second white piece for backing 16½ x 16½ inches. Cut 2 strips of fabric for border (red, green, or blue), two 2½ x 15½ inches and two 2½ x 18½ inches.

Trace the pattern pieces and assemble as for projects on pages 98 and 103. Cut out corresponding fusible webbing and center the appliqués on the front of the smaller square of fabric. Fuse with a hot iron. If desired, stitch around the edges of the appliqué with a zigzag stitch in a matching thread color.

With right sides facing and edges aligned, stitch the short border strips to opposite sides of the pillow front. Repeat on the other edges with long strips. Open and press seams.

Pin the straight edge of eyelet to the raw edge of the pillow front and stitch together. Pin the backing piece to the pillow front with the eyelet between. Stitch together from the back using the previously stitched line as a guide. Leave a few inches open on one side for turning.

Turn the pillow right side out and stuff or insert a pillow form. Stitch the opening closed with a slipstitch.

Pattern for four flowers pillow

Use diagonal, vertical, and horizontal creases to position pattern pieces on pillow squares.

Use template A to make pattern pieces for Peony pillow above.

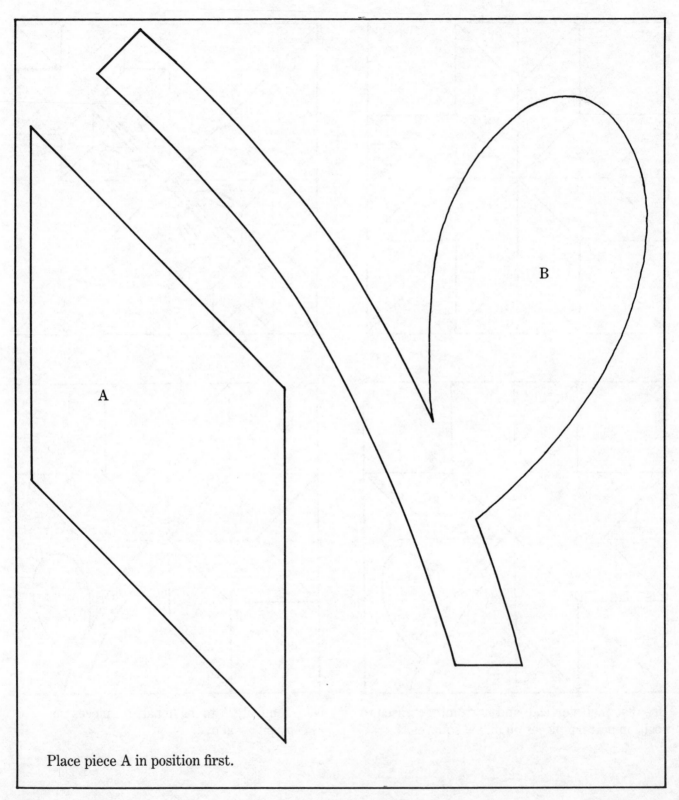

A

B

Place piece A in position first.

Peony pillow

Log cabin quilt

Use all the most beautiful scraps you have for a real old-fashioned log cabin coverlet. This one is 70 inches square and consists of one large pattern rather than a series of joined log cabin squares. I used scraps of Laura Ashley fabric for this project.

Materials: Quilt batting 70 x 70 inches; backing fabric (can be a sheet); and the following fabrics:
A (border and center) 1½ yards
B (border) 2 yards
C (beige color) ⅔ yard
D (blue color) ½ yard
E (green color) ⅓ yard
F (rust color) ½ yard

Directions
Cut the following and add ¼-inch seam allowance. Number of each fabric to be cut is indicated in parentheses.
A: 7 x 7 inches (1)
    16 x 42 inches (2)
B: 16 x 70 inches (2)
C: 3½ x 14 inches (2)
    3½ x 21 inches (2)
    3½ x 28 inches (2)
    3½ x 35 inches (2)
D: 3½ x 14 inches (2)
    3½ x 42 inches (2)
E: 3½ x 28 inches (2)
F: 3½ x 7 inches (2)
    3½ x 21 inches (2)
    3½ x 35 inches (2)

Quilt top assembly
With right sides facing and top edges aligned, leave ¼-inch seam allowance and stitch one 3½ x 7–inch F piece to the 7 x 7–inch A center. Repeat on bottom edge. Open seams and press. Attach side pieces D (3½ x 14 inches) to center A in the same way.
Follow the diagram to add each quilt strip.

Quilting
Cut the backing to the same size as the quilt top. Baste 3 layers together, with 70 x 70 inch batting between. Stitch along all seam lines to quilt. Do not stitch all the way to the edges; leave ½ inch for turning under.

Finish
Fold raw edges of top and backing in ½ inch and pin all around. Stitch around outside edges to finish.

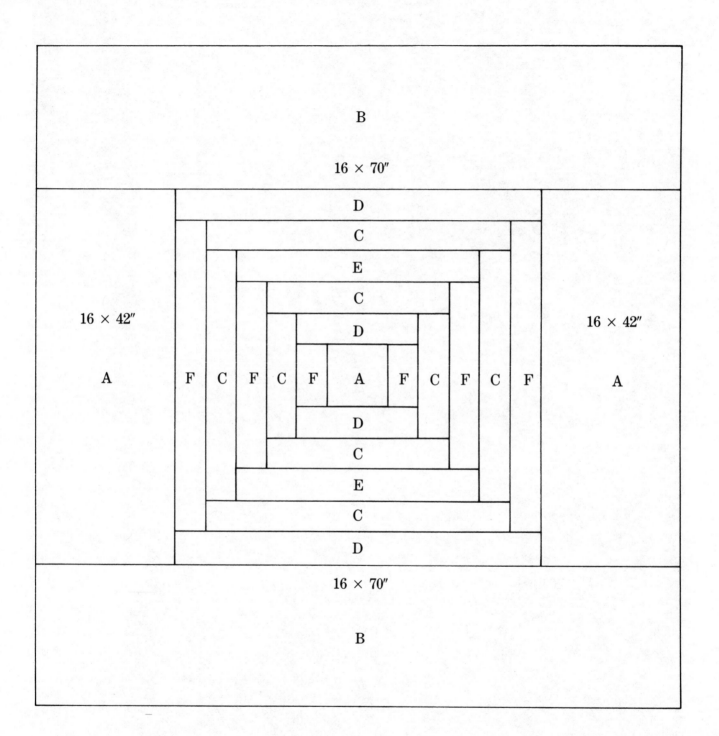

Stitchin' and stuffin'

Many of the projects in the following chapter require basic sewing skills, and anyone who can work a sewing machine will be able to complete the items in an evening. There are also pillows of many shapes and sizes. These require stitching and stuffing, and the following tips will help make them easier to do.

When cutting out shapes such as the animal pillows, for example, trace and transfer the shapes and specific facial details to the fabric. Muslin is an excellent background for these items, but you can also use printed cotton such as calico. The fabric for stuffed pillows should not be too thin.

When sewing around curved areas such as the rounded fruit pillows or the body of the animals, trim away excess material from the seam allowance and clip in to the seam line before turning. When sewing pointed areas, such as the ear on the cat (page 130), clip at either side of the ear where it meets the body. This will avoid bunching.

When stuffing these items and the corners of pillows, place small amounts of loose polyfil in the points and keep adding more stuffing a little at a time until full. To help get into the very points, use a crochet hook or end of an artist's paintbrush to push the stuffing to the end.

When sewing around the edges of a pillow, stitch around all 4 corners, leaving the center of one side open for turning. In this way all the corners will match.

Accent pillows

Take scraps of floral chintz and make these small accent pillows. One is 14 x 14 inches, the others are 12 x 12 inches. One of the small pillows has a rolled, padded border for interest, the other has a trapunto appliqué that is outlined with a zigzag stitch. The larger pillow has an appliquéd scene made from cut-out flowers fused to a solid background. The edge is scalloped and finished with a zigzag stitch. They are all easy projects to complete in an evening.

Trapunto appliqué pillow

Materials: Cut-out floral design; fusible webbing; 2 pieces of solid fabric 13 x 13 inches; 10 x 10 inch quilt batting; polyfil stuffing; 1 yard contrasting welting.

Directions

Pin the cut-out floral design to a piece of fusible webbing and cut around the outline. Center this on the front of one fabric piece and fuse together with a hot iron.

With the appliqué side up, pin the fabric to the quilt batting and machine-stitch around the appliqué with a contrasting zigzag stitch. With fabric face down, slit through the quilt batting on the underside of the appliqué and stuff with polyfil. Use a blunt instrument such as a crochet hook or artist's paintbrush handle to push the stuffing into points of leaves and hard-to-get-at areas.

With right sides facing, pin the raw edge of the welting around all 4 sides of the pillow and stitch together. Place the backing piece face down over the front piece and stitch around 3 sides, following the welting stitch line. Turn right side out and stuff. Close with a slipstitch.

Rolled border pillow

Materials: A pencil; ruler; 2 pieces of floral chintz or cotton 13 x 13 inches; polyfil stuffing.

Directions

With right side up, draw an 11-inch square on one piece of fabric. With right sides of the 2 fabric squares facing, stitch around 3 sides and 4 corners, leaving a ¼-inch seam allowance. Turn right side out and press.

Create a roll of stuffing to fit snugly around the inside seam line and pin the pillow along the drawn pencil line. The stuffing should remain between the pencil line and outside stitching. Do not stuff the open side at this time.

Stitch along the drawn line on the front of the fabric, leaving the opening free. Stuff the center of the pillow with polyfil and stitch along the open side on the pencil line (see diagram).

Add stuffing to the open border area on the fourth side and slipstitch closed. (This pillow can be made as a sachet. In this case you would fill it with potpourri or pine needles instead of the polyfil.)

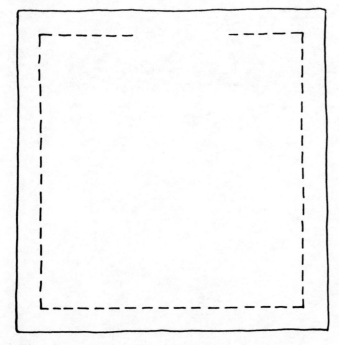

Pattern for scallop edge

Scalloped edge pillow

Materials: ½ yard solid fabric; a pencil and ruler; scrap of printed floral fabric; polyfil stuffing or 14 x 14–inch pillow form; fusible webbing.

Directions

Cut 2 squares of solid fabric 18 x 18 inches. With right side up, draw a 14½-inch square on one piece of fabric. Pin front and back pieces together. Using a 3-inch-diameter object like a jar or water glass, draw around the outside of the penciled outline to create a scalloped edge.

Place the printed floral fabric over the fusible webbing and pin together. Cut out each design element and arrange on the front of the pillow fabric. Fuse with a hot iron.

Use thread that matches the background fabric color and a zigzag stitch around the drawn scallops on the double layer of fabric, leaving one side open. Next, straight-stitch along 3 sides of the drawn square inside the scalloped edge.

With small snipping scissors, cut away excess fabric around the scallops as close to the stitch line as possible. Do not cut away the fabric on the fourth side.

Insert the pillow form, or stuff the pillow and pin the fabric along the remaining pencil line. Machine-stitch closed. Stitch with a zigzag around the remaining scallops and trim away excess fabric. Press the border and lightly press over the appliqué to secure any loose edges.

Harlequin screen

A room-divider screen is a functional as well as interesting backdrop in any room. This one opens to 4 panels, and no hardware is necessary. You sew a backing to the patched front and then stitch 3 seams down the center to create 4 pockets. Then insert pieces of ½-inch-thick Fomecore into each one. This creates a sturdy sound barrier that is as light as a feather for easy moving or storing away when not needed.

Materials: 3½ yards 45-inch-wide fabric for main color; scraps of solid colors to make 96 patches each 6½ inches square; 4 yards 52-inch-wide muslin for backing; four 24 x 66–inch Fomecore panels (available in art stores).

Directions

From the main color cut 117 patches 6½ inches square. From the other colors cut equal numbers of 6½-inch squares to total 96 patches.

With right sides facing and edges aligned, leave ¼ inch and seam together 3 patches according to the diagram. Open and press the seams. Continue to make 19 horizontal rows, graduating from 3 patches in a row to 17 patches in a row (see diagram for correct number of patches and order of each row).

Seam the rows together vertically. Add one patch at the top and bottom to complete the piece. Cut the rectangle as shown so that the border squares are now triangles all around the edge. The finished piece is approximately 68 x 102 inches.

Cut the muslin in half to create 2 pieces 52 x 72 inches. Stitch together to create one piece 72 x 104 inches. Trim to the same size as the front piece. With the right sides facing, stitch front and back together around the top and side edges, leaving the long bottom edge open. Turn right side out and press.

Measure and mark 3 lines at 25½-inch spaces. Pin and stitch through both layers of fabric along the marked lines. Slide each Fomecore panel into the 4 pockets. Turn in the open edges at the bottom and slipstitch.

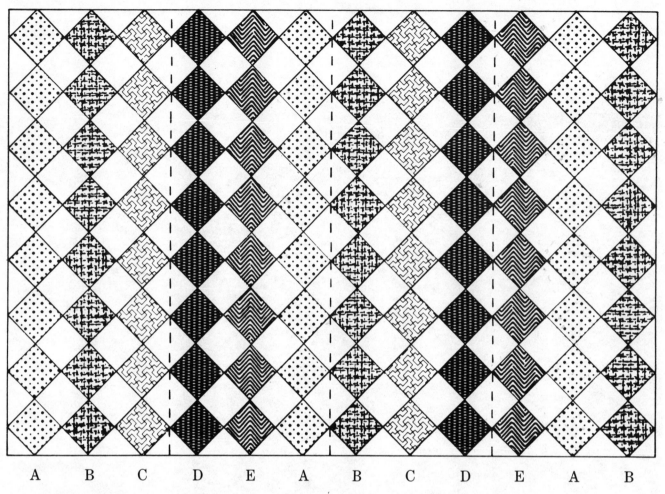

A B C D E A B C D E A B

Color sequence

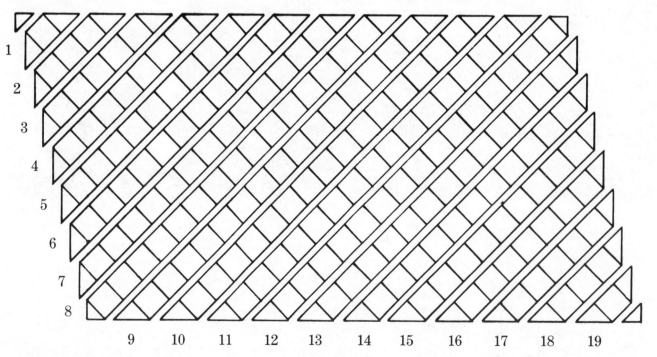

Patching sequence

122

All you need to make these plump fruit pillows are basic sewing skills. You piece them together from scraps of calico and plaids in the appropriate colors. Apple, pear, and strawberry shapes make a nice grouping.

Materials: Scraps of red, green, and yellow fabric; polyfil stuffing.

Directions

Enlarge each pattern piece (see page 14) and cut from scrap fabric pieces. The pear is made up of 3 different yellow patterns, the apple and strawberry from different reds. Each leaf and stem is cut from a different green calico print.

Follow the diagram to make the top of each pillow. Leave ¼-inch seam allowance. For added interest you can use a zigzag stitch around each point of the strawberry leaves.

Cut out a pillow back to match the pillow front. With right sides facing, seam front and back together, leaving 2 to 3 inches open at the center top edge. Clip into the seam allowance all the way around the curved edges. Turn right side out and stuff very full.

Stems

Cut 2 pieces for the apple and pear stems and seam each pair with right sides together except at the lower edge of each stem. Turn right side out and stuff.

Slip the stem into the top opening of each pillow. Slipstitch the open edges closed over the raw edges of the stem.

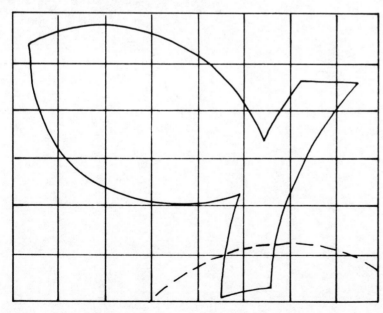

Each square equals 1″.

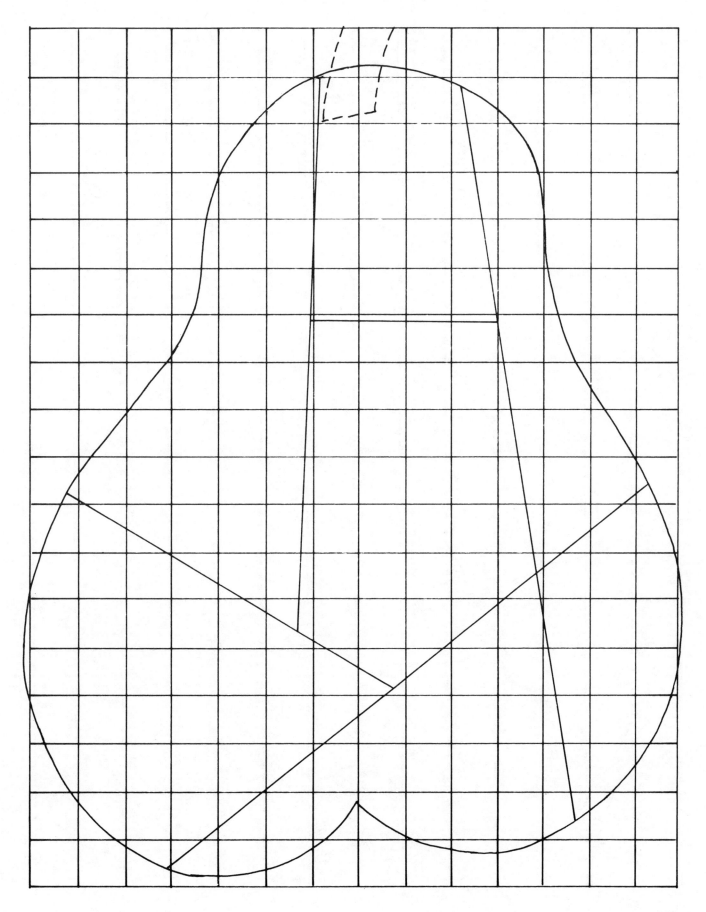

125

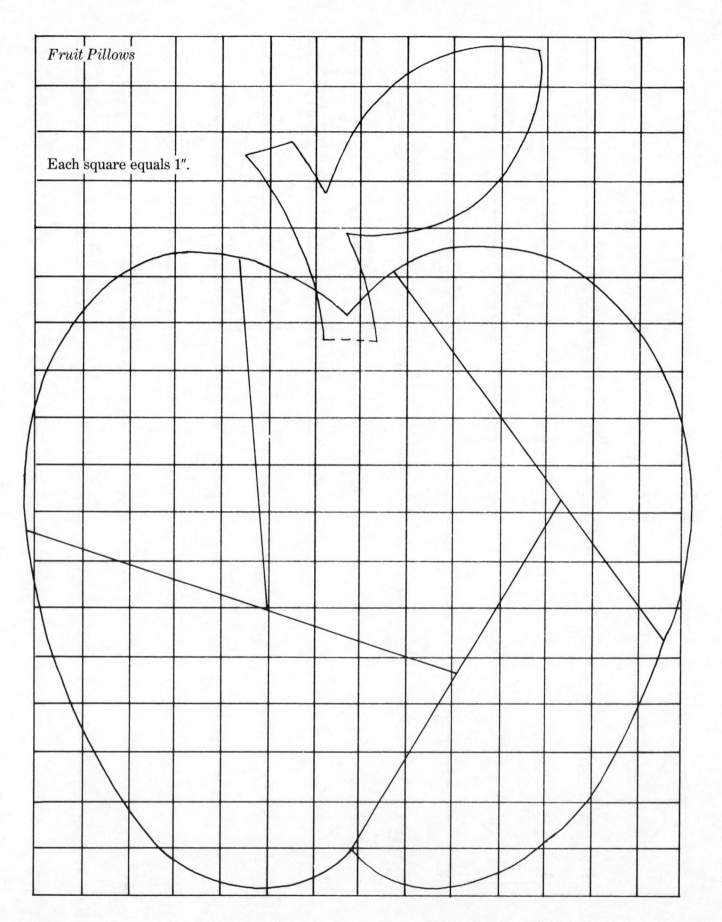

Fruit Pillows

Each square equals 1″.

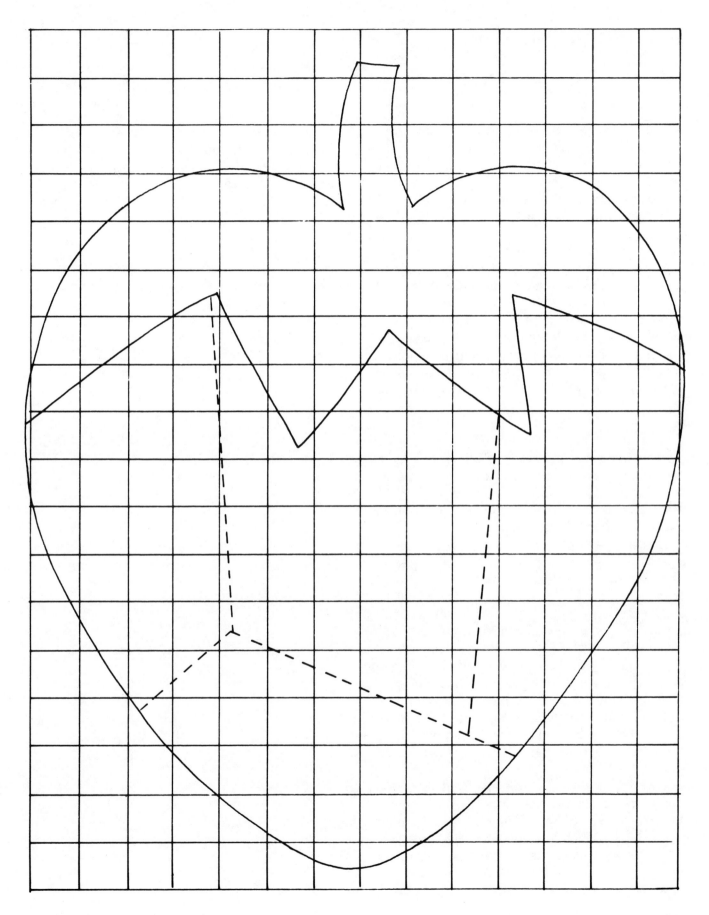

Animal pillows

Early American quilters would often make soft toys from scraps of fabric pieced together and sewn into animal shapes. Today antique shops often carry these pillow toys, which have been made from frayed and discarded pieces of quilts. They are quite expensive and prized for their country charm. It is not difficult to duplicate these items using your own leftovers. And who knows—they might become heirlooms that your great-grandchildren find in your attic.

Materials: ⅜ yard 45-inch-wide muslin for each pillow; scraps of printed pastel fabric; pencil and ruler; fusible webbing; quilt batting (optional); stuffing; paper punch (optional); small round black piece of fabric or waterproof marker for eye.

Directions

Trace each pattern shape. Fold the muslin in half and pin the pattern onto the muslin. Add ¼ inch for seam allowance and cut out two pieces for each pillow. Cut 2-inch squares of assorted pastel prints and fusible webbing.

Lightly mark diagonal lines spaced 2 inches apart across one body piece. Mark lines across in the opposite direction to create squares of 2 inches.

Alternating every other square, pin a fabric square with corresponding fusible webbing to the muslin. Fuse with a hot iron. For the hen, cut out and iron on a yellow beak. Edgestitch or zigzag stitch the raw edges of the patches and beak of the muslin to secure, if desired.

If you would like to quilt the body, cut a piece of quilt batting the same size as the front. Pin to the back of the body and stitch along the penciled lines.

With right sides of the body front and back facing, stitch around the edges, leaving about 3 inches open at the bottom edge. Clip around all edges to the stitch line and turn right side out. Stuff, using a blunt instrument like the eraser end of a pencil to push the stuffing into ears and other small areas. Slipstitch the opening closed.

Use a paper punch to cut out an eye from black fabric and fusible webbing, or use a black waterproof marker. Fuse to pillow. For the cat, cut an ear and fuse in place.

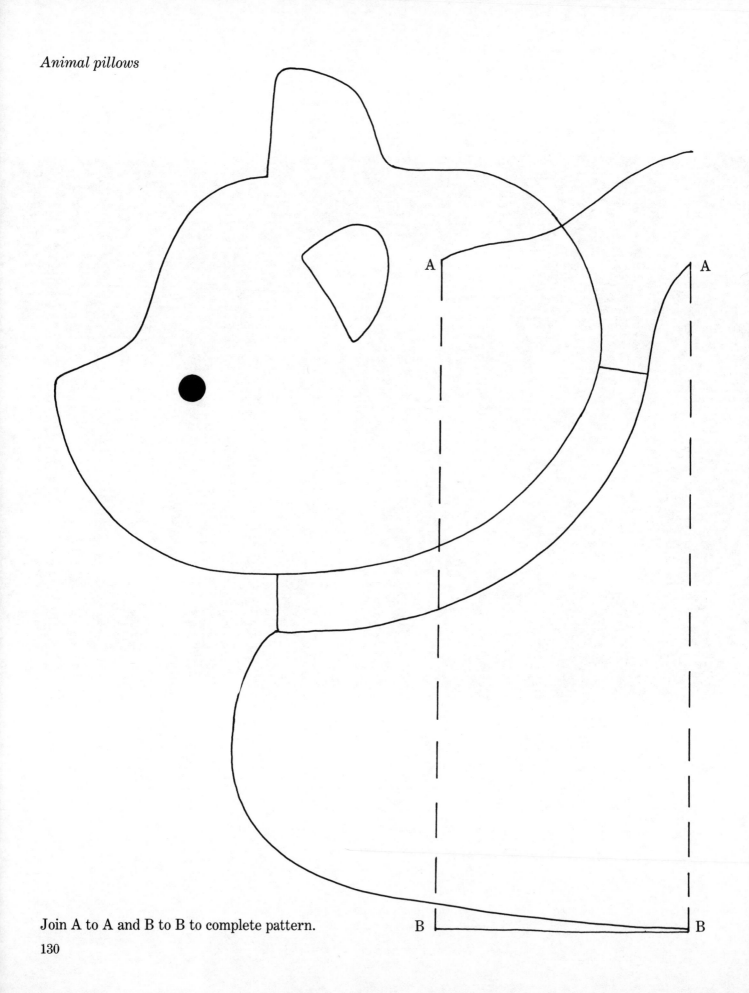

A

A

B   B

Join A to A and B to B to complete pattern.

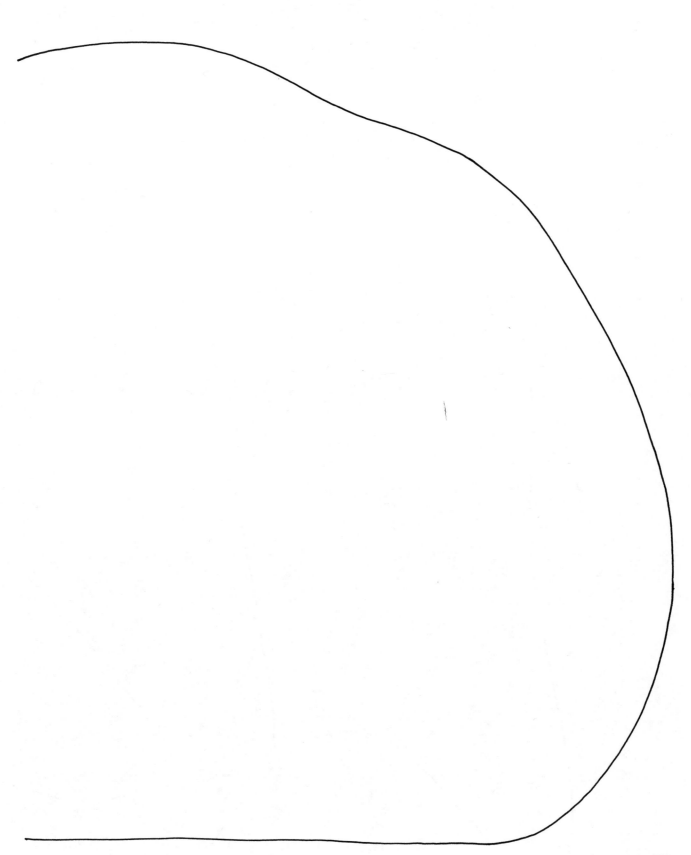

131

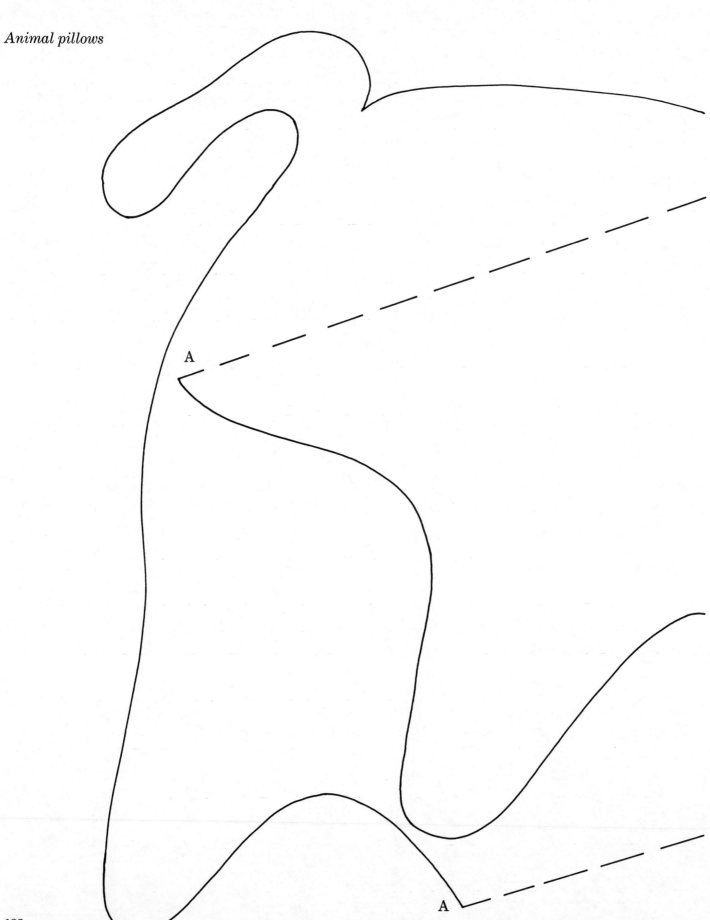

A

A

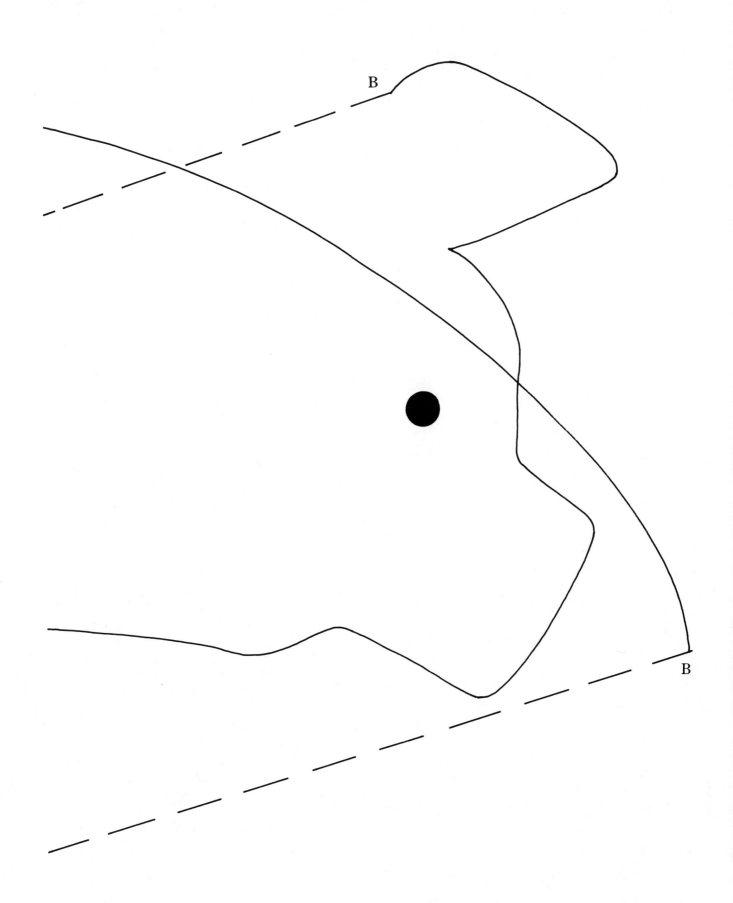

B

B

Join A to A and B to B to complete pattern.

133

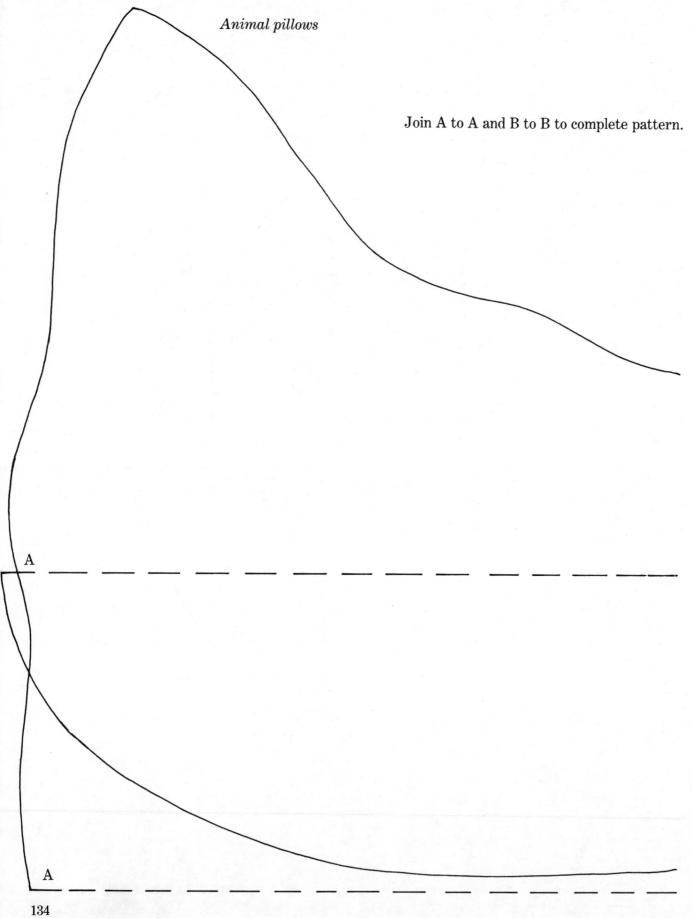

Animal pillows

Join A to A and B to B to complete pattern.

A

A

134

B

B

Delectable mountain tablecloth

This popular quilt pattern is delightful on top of a table cover. It can be pieced and quilted, or simply fuse the appliqué to a muslin background with fusible webbing. Use any color combination, but this red, white, and blue design is very Early American. The finished project is 54 inches square, but the design can be used on any size tablecloth.

Materials: 1½ yards muslin; ½ yard each of blue and red cotton fabric; fusible webbing; a pencil and tracing paper.

Directions

Cut a muslin square to fit the top of your table. Cut 4 strips of red fabric 2½ inches wide by the length of each side of the muslin. Cut a red square 7 x 7 inches. Cut a piece of fusible webbing the same size.

Enlarge the pattern pieces and trace onto a sheet of tracing paper. Use this to cut the Delectable Mountain designs from blue fabric, with a corresponding piece of fusible webbing. Follow the diagram and fuse the red square to the center of the muslin with a hot iron. Apply the blue pieces in the same way.

With right sides facing, stitch the red border strips to the edge of the tablecloth. Trim, if necessary, and turn the raw edges under ½ inch and hem.

137

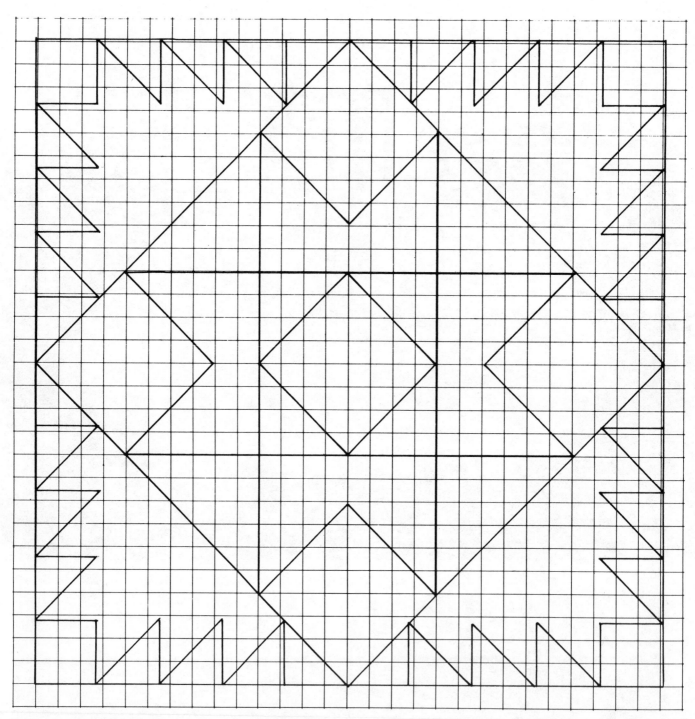

Each square equals 1″ for a 54″ square tablecloth.

Basket full of strawberries

Make a basket filled with large and small strawberry pillows from scraps of different red prints. Place the basket in a hallway for a cheerful greeting or make the little strawberries for Christmas ornaments. They're fun to make in bunches, and when filled with potpourri they make a lasting gift to use year round. Each pillow is 11 inches long and 13½ inches across.

Materials: ½ yard fabric for pillow; scraps of red printed fabric for sachets; ½ yard of green velveteen or corduroy for leaves and stems; brown wrapping paper; piece of white chalk; polyfil stuffing and potpourri mix for sachets; pinking shears; black ballpoint pen; ribbon for hanging.

Directions

When selecting fabric, look for calico, gingham, or a tiny print in red or pink colors. Solids are less interesting. The stem and leaves are cut from a plush, textured material, or, if you prefer, these can be cut from a green calico or other small print like gingham.

Enlarge pattern (see page 14) and transfer to a piece of brown wrapping paper. Pin this to the fabric and draw around it with white chalk. Cut two pieces.

With right sides facing, stitch around the strawberry, leaving a 3½-inch opening at the top. Clip around all curved edges to the seam line. Turn right side out and press.

Cut 2 pieces for the stem and 10 leaf pieces. With right sides facing, stitch around the stem edges, leaving the bottom edge open. Stitch each of the leaves in the same way, leaving a 1½-inch opening at the side of one point. Clip edges. Turn right side out.

Stuff the pillow so it is very full. Stuff the stem and stitch across the bottom. Using a needle and thread, gather the opening around the top of the strawberry opening so there is enough room to stuff the end of the stem into the hole. Insert one end of the stem and stitch together.

Each square equals 1″.

Stuff each of the leaves so they are full but not too plump. Slipstitch the opening of each leaf closed. Set the sewing machine for a basting stitch and run the machine down the center of each leaf to quilt it. The stitches should stop short of the top of each leaf to represent the vein. Stitch the leaves to the stem, pushing them down as close to the body as possible.

Sachet

Cut 2 pattern pieces for the sachet. Stitch as for the pillow. Stuff three-fourths full and fill the rest of the way with a mixture of long-grain rice, ground cloves, cinnamon, and a drop of strawberry oil.

Cut the leaves with pinking shears and draw veins on each leaf with a black ballpoint pen. Do not use markers as they may bleed on the fabric.

For hanging

Cut a 2½-inch piece of satin or grosgrain ribbon, fold it in half and stitch to the base of the stem. Tack each of the leaves around the stem.

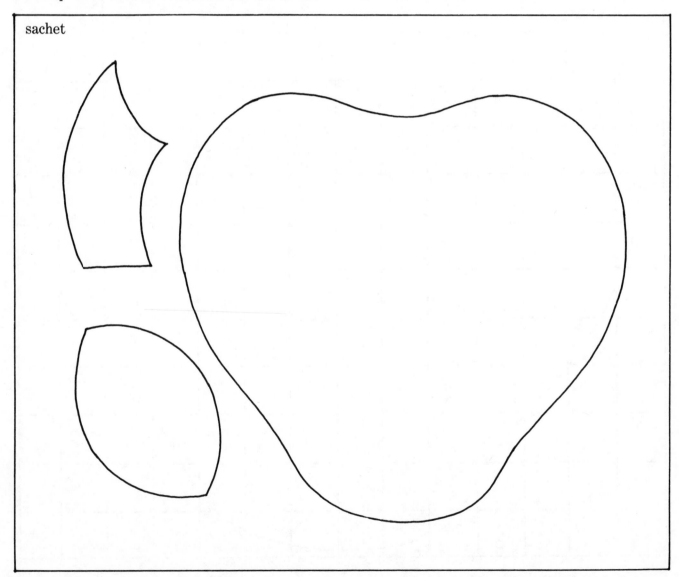

sachet

No-sew fabric projects

There are lots of fabric projects that require little or no sewing. These projects use materials such as iron-on seam binding, and fusible webbing like Stacy's Stitch Witchery, and make it possible to complete a project in an hour or two.

The apple picture on page 148 and the summer scene collage on page 151 are good examples of this. The fabric pieces are small and would be difficult to sew. Also, since they are pictures made with fabric, the sewing is not necessary. The decoupage plant pedestals on page 145 utilize cut-out floral fabric scraps in another way. In this case the fabric is either fused to the wood or glued in place.

Fabric shops also carry bonded fabrics in different colors. This fabric is much like contact paper in that you peel away the backing and stick the adhesive-backed fabric to another fabric to create appliquéd scenes. This is excellent for creating projects such as decorative lampshades, designs on a baby's crib or on a window shade.

Once you use some of these shortcut products for your crafting, you can whip up a gift or bazaar item in no time, and the results will be as good as those achieved with hours of crafting time.

Flowering plant pedestals

Pedestals can create varying heights for displaying plants, baskets, pottery, or pieces of art. If you can't find the exact size needed it's easy to make your own. You can also use unfinished cubes.

The surfaces are decorated with cut-out fabric flowers from a remnant of chintz and applied to the wood with fusible webbing. This is a good way to use beautiful scraps from draperies or slipcovers. These pedestals are 24 and 30 inches high and 12 inches square.

Materials: From the lumberyard have the following pieces cut for a *24 inch pedestal*: 4 pieces of 24-inch-long 1 x 12–inch pine; 2 pieces ¼-inch plywood 12 inches square. *For a 30 inch pedestal* you will need: 4 pieces 30-inches-long 1 x 12–inch pine; 2 pieces ¼-inch plywood 12 inches square. *For both pedestals:* White glue; 2-inch finishing nails (48 for each); wood filler to cover nail holes; medium sandpaper; all-purpose primer paint; latex or enamel paint (1 quart for 2 pedestals); 2-inch sponge brush; clear spray varnish (optional).

Tools: Hammer; nail set (available in hardware stores); putty knife.

Materials needed for decoupage: Remnant of floral fabric; fusible webbing; small scissors.

Directions for pedestals

Spread glue along the cut ends of each pine piece to be glued together, to create the 4 sides of the pedestal.

Assemble the 4 pieces so the top and bottom are lined up and you have created a hollow box. Press the glued pieces together and let dry thoroughly. This is important in order to create a solid object.

Nail each overlapping corner on 4 sides at the top and the bottom. Place 2 more nails evenly spaced on each side between top and bottom.

Spread glue around the top edge of the pedestal and set 1 piece of ¼-inch plywood over the

glued top edges. Let dry thoroughly. Hammer a nail at each corner edge and 2 more evenly spaced between each corner on the top. Turn the pedestal upside down and repeat on the bottom. Let dry thoroughly.

Set all nails with the nail set. (This is a little metal piece that you place over the nail head and simply hammer to sink the nail below the surface of the wood.) Fill each hole with wood filler. If there are any imperfections in the wood surface, you can use the putty knife to spread some wood filler over these areas. Let the filler dry. Sand the wood-filled areas with medium sandpaper to smooth the surface, if needed.

To finish

Give the entire unit a coat of primer and let dry. Sand lightly. Apply 2 coats of paint, letting each dry thoroughly.

Directions for decoupage

Traditionally, decoupage is the craft of cutting out and applying paper designs. However, for these projects I found some wonderful floral chintz and cut out and rearranged the designs to suit the pedestals.

Pin your fabric to fusible webbing and cut out each element. Small snipping or cuticle scissors are useful for getting at small areas such as between leaves and stems, and so on.

Arrange the design on one side of the pedestal and stand back. Decide what designs you will put on the side that butts against it so your pattern will be continuous and flow nicely. You may only want to decorate two sides. Once the designs have been worked out, you will fuse each piece to the painted surface with a hot iron. To do this, be careful not to allow the hot iron to touch the paint directly. Latex paint wil bubble and peel if it gets too hot. If this should happen, press the paint down with your palm and let it dry. If it lifts, add a leaf or bud over the spoiled area or wait until the project is finished and touch up with paint.

Continue to press small areas of fabric to the

pedestal until it is entirely covered. Another way to apply the cutouts is by glueing them all in place with white glue. The glue will be secure and binding. It takes a little longer this way, and it's messier, but it's more foolproof.

To protect the surface you might want to give the entire pedestal a coating of clear spray varnish.

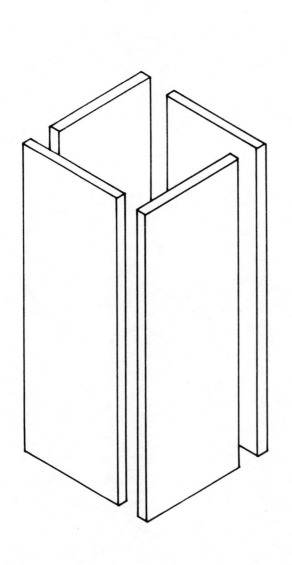

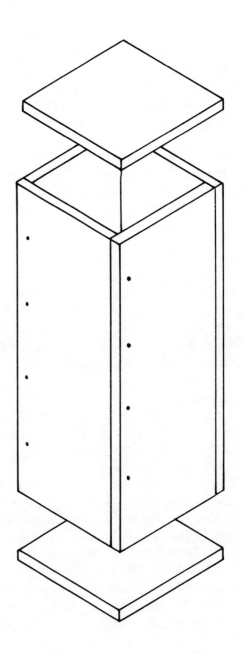

Apple picture

This appliqué picture is created without the usual work involved with appliqués. Each apple is created with scraps of fabric and fusible webbing for a delightful country picture. Hang it in your kitchen or family room to brighten any wall. The finished size is 20 x 22 inches.

Materials: ¾ yard muslin; ¼ yard 45-inch-wide dark blue print for the border; fusible webbing; pencil, tracing paper, and thin cardboard; scraps of red and green fabric; 20 x 22 inch frame and backing.

Directions

Draw a rectangle 20 x 22 inches on the muslin. Cut 4 strips of dark blue fabric 2½ x 22 inches and 4 matching strips of fusible webbing. Arrange the border strips along the inside of the drawn lines with the webbing between the fabric and the muslin. The corners will overlap.

Trace the apple pattern and transfer to thin cardboard such as a manilla folder. Cut out and use this as a template to draw 16 apples on the red and green scrap fabric pieces. Pin each fabric piece to fusible webbing and cut out. Cut 16 leaves and stems the same way.

Mark off 4 evenly spaced rows across and down on the muslin, using a pencil dot or pin to indicate lines. Arrange the apples so you have 4 rows of 4 on the muslin and fuse with a hot iron. Fuse a leaf and stem with each apple.

Cut the muslin about 2 inches outside the blue borders. Spread the picture over the frame backing and pull the extra muslin to the back. Use masking tape to hold in place and frame the picture.

Apple picture

Create this pastoral summer scene with small bits of fabric and fusible webbing. Then add a nice frame and you have an easy, inexpensive-to-make picture for any room. This is a nice way to give a personalized gift. You can design something that represents the person you will give it to. The finished size is 9½ x 20 inches.

Materials: Fusible webbing; piece of light blue fabric 10 x 20 inches; variety of scrap fabric pieces; 10 x 20 inch frame; pencil and tracing paper; paper punch.

Directions

Cut a piece of fusible webbing the same size as the blue fabric and place both pieces over the frame backing. Fuse with a hot iron.

Trace pattern pieces and pin each to a corresponding piece of fabric. Before cutting out, pin the fabric to fusible webbing and cut through both layers. Cut a piece of dark blue fabric with fusible webbing the same size for the water area. Fuse in place at the lower right hand corner of the picture.

Cut green hills and fuse them to the left hand corner. Arrange cut-out fabric pieces for houses, boats, pier, lighthouse, bushes, clouds, and sun in place on background. The fruit on the trees is cut with a paper punch. Fuse all appliqués in place with a hot iron. Frame and hang.

153

154

Sewing caddy

A sewing caddy may not be a decorating item, but it's handy to have for all the sewing projects you'll be doing. This was made with leftover fabric scraps and an empty ice cream container. It's pretty as well as useful, so it can be left out on your sewing table for looks and convenience.

Materials: Small piece of colorful fabric; empty plastic ice cream or yoghurt container; pencil; polyfil stuffing; glue; 1-inch-wide satin ribbon.

Directions

Cut a piece of fabric wide enough to wrap around the base of the container with enough to tuck under the bottom. Cut another piece to fit over the bottom. Draw a circle on the fabric large enough to fit over the top when padded. Use a dessert plate or other round object as a template.

Spread white glue over the outside surface of the container base. Wrap the fabric around it and press down firmly. Clip in around the fabric that extends at the bottom where the container tapers in and fold and glue the fabric to the bottom. Glue the round bottom piece over the tucks.

Wad a mound of stuffing and glue to the top of the container. Place the top piece of fabric over the stuffing and glue to the inside of the top edge as you make gentle folds all around. Finish off the edge with a band of ribbon glued all around. Attach a few inches of ribbon by tacking it to one side of the lid and make a loop at the other end to hold a pair of scissors. The top becomes a pin cushion, while the inside holds all other sewing essentials like thread, buttons, pins, and so on.

Sources of supplies

Art supplies

Arthur Brown, Inc.
2 West 46th St.
New York, NY 10036

Charrette
31 Olympia Ave.
Woburn, MA 01801
(catalog $1)

Calico

The Weston Country Store
Weston, VT 05161

Embroidery hoops

Lee Wards Creative Crafts Ctr.
12 Saint Charles St.
Elgin, IL 60120

The Stitchery
Dept. 143
Wellesley, MA 02181

Herbs for potpourri

Caswell-Massey Co. Ltd.
518 Lexington Ave.
New York, NY 10017

Wide World of Herbs Ltd.
11 Catherine St. East
Montreal, 129 P. Quebec, Canada

Quilting fabrics

The Quilt Patch
261-D Main St.
Northern, MA 01532

Fabrications
100 Wells Ave.
Newton, MA 02159

Most of the supplies used for the projects in the book are familiar and can be found in most fabric or hobby shops, or art supply stores. However, I've listed a few sources for those specific items that may be difficult to locate and which can be purchased through mail order. If you have any trouble with any project or can't locate materials write to me and I will try to find a source.
Leslie Linsley
Nantucket, MA 02554